Get the Education You Deserve at a Price You Can Afford

THE COMPLETE GUIDE TO

D0034850

PAYING FOR COLLEGE

Save Money, Cut Costs, and Get More
for Your Education Dollar

LEAH INGRAM

Foreword by William J. Behre, PhD, Provost and Chief Academic Officer,
Georgian Court University

"In her latest book, *The Complete Guide to Paying for College*, Leah provides comprehensive information for students and parents on one of the most pressing financial issues of today. Her thorough coverage of the topic from a middle-class parent's perspective is both authentic and exceptionally informative."

—Clare K. Levison, CPA, author of *Frugal Isn't Cheap*

"I will be clutching this book tightly and referencing it often. Leah's proactive approach, practical solutions and thorough lists of questions to answer at each step of the way will help all those bound for college. Reading it will make you feel like you're sitting at Leah's kitchen table and she's walking you step by step through the process, while you sip on your favorite tea or coffee. She will prepare you for the higher education financial journey. A must read for all parents and headed to college."

—Erin Chase, author of $5 Dinner Mom Cookbook series

"*The Complete Guide to Paying For College* examines every nook and cranny of how to afford the high and soaring cost of higher education. Leah offers practical solutions and easy to understand explanations for the various funding mechanisms and expenses that students and parents will face during the college experience."

—Douglas A. Boneparth, CFP® and coauthor of *The Millennial Money Fix*

"Smartly paying for college without sacrificing your (or your child's) financial future can seem like an overwhelming task. You need a relevant, timely resource to help you put it all together. Thankfully, Leah Ingram has done just that in her new book. She covers it all—from justifying the expense of higher education to spending wisely while there. Grab this guide and feel confident that you've got an up-to-date, comprehensive tool to help you make the smartest financial decisions toward your college experience."

—Philip Taylor, FinCon founder

"This well-written and engaging book is a must-read for any parent who is worried about paying for college. If you're in the middle class, you often don't qualify for traditional financial aid. And trying to pay the sticker price for a degree isn't even a possibility. But now you have an easy-to-follow blueprint for financial survival during your kid's college years. Money-saving expert, Leah Ingram, offers insider tips that show you how to save money and still give your child a quality education. This book is a great resource and it deserves a permanent spot on your nightstand."

—Beverly Harzog, author, *Confessions of a Credit Junkie* and *The Debt Escape Plan*

"Any parent looking for help figuring out how to pay for college will want to read Leah Ingram's book. *The Complete Guide to Paying for College* offers smart tips to keep tuition bills down and find ways to pay them as well as ideas for the students to save on college expenses after they enroll. I wish I had known them all before my sons launched their undergraduate years."

—Richard Eisenberg, Money & Security Editor, PBS Nextavenue.org

Get the Education You Deserve
at a Price You Can Afford

THE COMPLETE GUIDE TO PAYING FOR COLLEGE

Save Money, Cut Costs, and Get More
for Your Education Dollar

LEAH INGRAM

Foreword by William J. Behre, PhD, Provost and
Chief Academic Officer,
Georgian Court University

CAREER
PRESS

Wayne, N.J.

THE COMPLETE GUIDE TO PAYING FOR COLLEGE
EDITED BY ROGER SHEETY
TYPESET BY KARA KUMPEL
Cover design by Rob Johnson/toprotype
Student photo by Andrey_Popov/shutterstock
Printed in the U.S.A.

To order this title, please call toll-free 1-800-CAREER-1 (NJ and Canada: 201-848-0310) to order using VISA or MasterCard, or for further information on books from Career Press.

CAREER
PRESS

The Career Press, Inc.
12 Parish Drive
Wayne, NJ 07470
www.careerpress.com

Library of Congress Cataloging-in-Publication Data

CIP Data Available Upon Request.

To Jane and Annie

Thank you for inspiring me to write this book.

Contents

Part III: Savings While in School

Foreword

When Leah and I got married in 1992, I was a middle school teacher in New York City's inner city. I grew up in a middle-class town in the suburbs and attended a prestigious liberal arts college. My education was worlds away from that of my students. The odds were against them completing high school, let alone going to college. That experience with those young people convinced me to go to graduate school to study education in order to better understand what struggles American youth face as they seek to further their educations. Not surprisingly, cost is a key impediment for many students.

Our family is fortunate. Leah and I make solid incomes. Still, having two children in college has put real stress on our household budget. That said, I've never been more convinced that this investment is worth it. The experience our daughters are gaining from being at college cannot be replicated. And, I'm not just talking about in-the-classroom experience. This year, for example, our older daughter is living with three women whose backgrounds couldn't be more different from her own suburban Pennsylvania upbringing. Her roommates are a Latina from the Bronx, a Cuban immigrant, and a Muslim woman from Tunisia. Our younger daughter, who is pursuing a degree in engineering, spent last summer at a camp on her college's campus, mentoring would-be young engineers. These interactions have exposed them to perspectives that you can't find in most other places. It has also opened them to career and learning options that they might never have considered. This expansion of possibility is the key reason I believe that college is worth it for most adolescents, despite its costs.

When they discuss the cost of college, many people limit its value to a simple financial return on investment. Will the student earn enough to justify the cost? Given the price tag, clearly, earnings have to be a consideration. And indeed, on average, college graduates earn substantially more than their non-college peers. But the conversation shouldn't end there. There is much more value in earning a college degree.

College-educated people are more likely to have other positive outcomes. They are less likely to get divorced. Researchers don't know for sure why this is, but there are some likely theories that help to explain this outcome.

First, college-educated people tend to marry a bit later than their non-college peers, and they are less likely to have children out of wedlock. This means that for college-educated people, marriage may be a more deliberate, planned-out act. Most colleges also focus on communication skills and problem-solving. Anyone who has been in a successful marriage can speak to the value of these skills in navigating a successful relationship. Finally, personal finance is one of the greatest stressors in a marriage. Having a higher earning potential, which college provides, creates a greater chance of having adequate financial resources, which reduces this stress.

College-educated people also tend to live longer. Different sources offer different longevity estimates, which range between seven and 10 years higher than non-college peers. Again, no one can be certain why this is. Surely job choice has something to do with it. Many dangerous jobs do not require college degrees. Other explanations include the fact that college graduates (presumably due at least in part to the analytical skills they learned in college) are less likely to engage in dangerous behaviors, such as smoking, driving without seatbelts, or skipping regular checkups. College graduates are also more likely to report being happy, volunteer, take part in civic activities, and donate to charity. Yes, many of these positive outcomes can be linked to income. However, it is also very possible that in 21st century America, the act of attending college creates a greater awareness of the interconnectedness of people and the need to engage in something that is bigger than one's self. It helps young people to determine what they stand for. And as the old cliché says, "If you don't stand for something, you are likely to fall for anything."

I've spent two decades now working with college students. I firmly believe in opportunities that a college degree offers. I want to see as many young people as possible take part in this journey of growth. In order for this to happen, they must figure out a way to afford it. This book can be an early step in a great adventure, whether you are a parent reading this for your child, or a student trying to figure things out on your own. College is the door to a world of fantastic opportunities. Figuring out how to pay for it is one of the keys to that door. Take pride in the sense of accomplishment that comes from forging that key.

William J. Behre, PhD

Introduction

Why the Middle Class
Needs This Book

Did you do that crazy college math that my husband and I did when our daughters were first born? You know, those calculations that went something like this: by the time our children are old enough to go to college, it's going to cost a quarter of a million dollars for four years of private college for each child? Even a state college education wouldn't be a bargain—easily clocking in north of $100,000.

If you were like us, after having done this math, you promptly set up a 529 plan college savings account for your children. You diligently sent money to these accounts, based on what you could afford out of current earnings. But then, perhaps a few years later, you got to the point where my husband and I got: we realized that we were facing a double-edged sword when it came to saving for college.

We were never going to be able to put away enough money to pay for what college was going to cost when our daughters were old enough to attend and, given our career choices, we were never going to be able to earn enough to fully seed those 529 accounts. In order to put away enough to pay for a private college (the kind of college my husband and I attended), in reality we needed to save $1,100 per month *per child* starting the month that child was born.

We have two children who were born just 23 months apart. So that meant starting in the year my eldest daughter turned two, we would have to be putting away at least $2,200 a month to pay for college.

As a young family in our early 30s, both early in our careers, that $2,200 a month—or $26,400 a year—was close to our take-home pay! We also had to cover housing, food, taxes, cars, and so on. Even if we'd wanted to put that much away, there is a limit to how much you can send to a 529 plan each year without incurring tax consequences. In fact, you are limited to putting $14,000 a year in a 529. Anything more than that and you get into gift tax territory. I won't bore you with the tax details, but suffice it to say, very early on, we realized that fully funding a 529 each year was completely unattainable, and we stopped trying.

Instead of covering what would be 100 percent of tuition in our monthly savings, we continued to send a reasonable amount to those 529 accounts so that we could cover some of their future college costs. Fast forward 18 years and the amount saved was enough to cover a few semesters of books for each child, but that was it.

Plenty of parents continue to use 529 plans to help sock away money for college. Those who are lucky enough to live in a few states can even prepay tuition. There used to be more than 20 states offering prepaid tuition plans—meaning you pay for college tomorrow at today's rates. Now, just a handful do.

After giving up on the dream of saving for a college education, we decided to put a different plan in place. It was our goal to find a way to pay for college using more reasonable strategies that made sense for a middle-class family like ours. That strategic thinking is what gave me the idea to write this book.

We knew we weren't alone in wanting a doable solution for paying for college, especially with the cost of college going up every year. I mean, the *combined* tuition bills for my husband's and my own college education didn't even come close to six figures. When I was a student at New York University, the salary my single mother earned was more than enough to cover *my entire* college tuition bill. I'm talking all four years. Today, my own income just barely covers *one year of one of my daughter's* college tuition bills.

College costs are straining everyone except the very rich.

On the other side of the income spectrum are needier families. There will always be help for them when their children go to college. For example, families whose total income adds up to $50,000 will nearly always qualify for significant need-based aid. In addition, the federal government is usually there to help out, such as with Pell Grants.

So that leaves the rest of us, the middle class, wondering how we're going to pay for college.

Pew Research says that 51 percent of American families are considered to be in the middle class.[1] That means we are the majority of U.S. citizens. And we're all in the same boat.

We are the ones facing some of the biggest challenges paying for college. We typically don't qualify for significant financial aid but, like with what happened with our family, we will not have saved enough to pay cash for college because we've never earned enough to be able to put that amount of money aside. If families are trying to put more than one child through college (like we are!), the challenges are exponential.

If you want your child to receive a quality education, but lack the income to pay today's college tuition out of pocket, this book is for you.

Readers want answers and advice, and they will get them. *The Complete Guide to Paying for College* is a step-by-step guide to every possible way to save on education costs and the many living expenses—room, board, books, activities—that come with it. *The Complete Guide to Paying for College* walks you through hundreds of actionable tips that apply year after year as school progresses. This book is written for students and parents trying to figure out how to pay for college.

I'm confident readers will find value in this book's suggestions regardless of how old their children are or what grade in school the student is. That's because the book includes advice for those wanting to plan years ahead, but it also includes ideas for students in their junior or senior year of high school. You might think there's no time left to find scholarships or other ways to cut the cost of college, but you would be wrong.

Because I have lived and am living the challenge of sending children to college, you can feel confident that the advice I'm sharing is authentic and based in the real world. I want to help you understand the basics of financing college, including financial aid and scholarships, a.k.a. the usual suspects. Another example of the usual suspects is community college. We've heard a lot about that lately, and many might believe that it is the savings salvation we've all been seeking when it comes to a college education. Trust me—it's definitely an option, but it's not the only one. I pride myself on the fact that this book uncovers little-known ways to pay for and get a college education.

This book covers so much territory. I offer a whole range of new savings that most other books on paying for college skip over *completely*—sibling discounts, employment options (read: work for a college, and your kid may go to college for free), ways to save on school materials, and how to avoid paying for college applications. I've also included profiles of creative ways other parents are saving and how students are getting their college education without going broke.

With all of these savings ideas, parents and students who have bought this book will quickly recoup the cost of their investment. With this evergreen advice, I promise you'll continue to save even more, before, during, and after college.

Paying for college is about to get easier.

I'm a family finance guru, a journalist, the wife of a college administrator, and the parent of two college-aged kids. I've cracked the code on paying for college, and what I've learned is here, in this must-have volume for every college-bound student and family.

One final note: *The Complete Guide to Paying for College* was finished during the transition of one federal administration to another. As such, there have been many changes—or anticipated changes—related to education since I finished writing this book. That's why if you visit *http://www.leahingram.com/category/paying-for-college/* you'll find the section called "Paying for College" on my blog.

It's in this section where I'll be publishing updated information on all things higher education, including, of course, news about paying for college. It's also where I'll be offering a free download to readers—a financial aid spreadsheet that I created and used to help both of my daughters find an affordable way to pay for college. I hope you'll stop by the blog and become a regular reader. It's going to be a great way for you to stay current on everything you need to know about paying for college.

Part I

Before the Applications

Chapter 1

Is College Worth It?

With how much college costs to attend these days, you or your parents may be wondering if getting a college education is even worth it. I understand that for some parents, like my husband and me, there is absolutely no question that a four-year degree is worth pursuing, regardless of how much that degree costs. For other parents, maybe yours, there are feelings of confusion about whether it's worth it to spend all that money on a piece of paper.

Perhaps your own parents did not get a four-year college degree. Or maybe they only have an associate's degree and, as far as they're concerned, they're doing just fine for themselves. In this chapter I'm going to present the benefits of a college degree from an earning, employment, and opportunity point of view. I'm hoping that this information will help affirm the value of a college degree so you can feel confident you're making the right decision as you begin to pursue higher education.

Jobs that require a college degree

If you aspire to be a doctor, dentist, or lawyer, then you probably already know that you need to get a college degree, along with at least one advanced degree. But did you know that some of the best-paying, non-legal jobs out there also require an advanced degree? And by "advanced" I mean a degree beyond your bachelor's.

Many jobs in healthcare require a master's degree. This includes nurse practitioner, physician's assistant, and nurse midwife. However, many other industries look for master's degrees as well. This includes math-related jobs (statistician and economist, for example) as well as education. In this latter group I'm not just talking about the people doing the teaching in both K-12 schools and at colleges and universities, but also those working in the administrative offices.

There are plenty of great-paying jobs that only require a bachelor's degree as well. Many of them are in the field of engineering, something a recent Georgetown University Public Policy Institute study titled "Recovery: Job Growth and Education Requirements Through 2020" confirms.[1] It says that along with healthcare and community service, jobs in STEM (science, technology, engineering, and mathematics) will be the fastest growing in our economy. Starting salaries in STEM can be close to six figures.

I don't want to bore you with lots of numbers, but I think these numbers make the case for getting a college education. In fact, that Georgetown University study reports that by 2020, 65 percent of all jobs in the economy will require postsecondary education and training beyond high school.

That breaks out to be the following:

⇨ 35 percent of the job openings will require at least a bachelor's degree

⇨ 30 percent of the job openings will require some college or an associate's degree

⇨ 36 percent of the job openings will not require education beyond high school

Sure, you could look at these statistics and think, well the greatest percentage of those jobs only require a high school diploma. That may be true, but if you lump together the job opportunities beyond high school, you're looking at 65 percent of the job opportunities. So why would you limit yourself to one-third of the opportunities when you could make yourself available to the possibility of two-thirds of those employment opportunities?

One last thing to consider from this Georgetown University study: those that will find the greatest opportunities for employment must possess certain desirable skills. These skills are the ones that any higher-education expert will explain you're more likely to develop, having gone to college. We're not talking hands-on skills, but skills such as:

↪ critical thinking

↪ active listening

↪ mathematical knowledge

↪ oral comprehension and expression

When you attend lectures, participate in small-group discussions, and take a variety of classes at college, you're more likely to develop these four highly valued skills. That makes you more competitive in the job market and potentially earns you a higher salary.

College degree and income gaps

Speaking of salaries, it's a well-known fact that there is an income gap between those with a college degree and those without one. In fact, as time goes on, that gap continues to widen.

Consider this latest study from Pew Research. It showed that Millennials with a college degree, ages 25 to 32, were earning, on average, $17,500 *more* than their classmates with just a high school diploma. Those with only some college or a two-year degree didn't fare much better. They're earning $15,500 *less* than their peers with a four-year degree, putting them only $2,000 above those with just a high school diploma.[2]

I know it's hard to even think ahead to your being a person in his mid-20s, working full-time, and worrying about a salary. But the truth is you can't avoid the topic of who you might be in the future. I mean, the whole idea for going to college and getting a college degree is to become the best version of yourself, including optimizing your earning potential in your future employment.

There's likely another reason there is such a big income gap between levels of education. It's simply easier for a college graduate to get a higher-paying job. You'll find this notion reflected in recent Bureau of Labor Statistics (BLS) numbers.[3] It shows the stark difference in the unemployment rate, based on education.

The overall unemployment rate for everyone over age 25 is 3.9 percent. However, that number changes quite a bit when you break it down by level of education. Here is the percentage of the population that is unemployed, based on education, and based on the most recent BLS numbers:

↪ Some high school: 7.9 percent

↪ High school diploma: 5.1 percent

↪ Some college/two-year degree: 3.8 percent

↪ Bachelor's degree and higher: 2.5 percent

So that's two checks in the win column for going to college. In addition to gaining the ability to earn more money in your career, these numbers show that you are more likely to avoid being unemployed because you have a bachelor's degree.

Networking opportunities through a college degree

Here's another leg up that going to college gives you— an alumni network. Think about it this way: every person who graduated before you at your college or university could potentially employ you. One study showed that nine out of 10 college graduates would hire someone who went to the same school that they did.[4] Nine out of 10. That's 90 percent.

This isn't just me talking. The Princeton Review has a publication called *Colleges That Pay You Back*. The idea is that these are the schools that your investment in getting a degree there will pay you back exponentially with time. One of the ways that payback happens is through employment. Sure, the colleges on this list are the ones you expect to hear (read: Ivy Leagues). Surprisingly, though, smaller colleges also make the cut, such as New College of Florida and Hampden-Sydney in Virginia, as do many public universities, including the University of Georgia, Florida State University, and Texas A&M.

The great thing about having an alumni network is that you never know when it is going to come in handy, but at least it's there for you. One of the places you can work your alumni network is on social media, especially LinkedIn. If you haven't yet checked out this work-related social networking site, you should at least have a profile up on LinkedIn by the time you're a freshman in college.

I can tell you from firsthand experience that there is a benefit to being on LinkedIn. Even better is having where I went to college (New York University or NYU) in my bio. I've also joined groups on LinkedIn related to NYU, which has led to paying work.

Don't believe me about alumni networks and the importance of getting a job after college? When you eventually make a campus visit, go on a college tour, or sit in on a college information session, find out how *successful* the school's graduates are and how successful the college is in getting them employed. "Are graduates getting a job, in what field, and what kind of success are they having," suggests Justin G. Roy, dean of admissions at Georgian Court University in Lakewood, New Jersey. "You want to find out about their earnings, job retention five years out, and their satisfaction rankings." If you are looking at a college with a 70 percent job placement rate versus a college with a 90 percent job placement rate, adds Roy, "It might be worth the investment of more money to go to the school with the 90 percent job placement rate."

If the ultimate goal of going to college is to make you better prepared to get a better-paying job, you want to ensure that a college can help you do that. Ask about its alumni network. Pop into the career services office and see what they can tell you about how they help graduates. Find out what percentage of graduates give money to their college. A recent survey found that 80 percent of donors give money because they believe their association with their alma mater has helped them professionally.[5] So the rate that graduates give is often a clue as to how engaged (or not engaged) they are with their school and how satisfied (or unsatisfied) they were with their college experience.

This is all a way of saying that, though college may be expensive, overall it is a very good investment for your future. This is especially true if you aspire to work in an industry that requires at least a bachelor's degree.

That said, I do understand that college is expensive. Remember: I have two daughters in college right now. In order to cover their tuition, housing, fees, and other expenses, our family is using a combination of earnings (my husband's, mine, and my daughters' from their summer and on-campus jobs), scholarships, grants, and loans. True, my daughters will graduate with debt like many American college students do, but the debt will not be so overwhelming that they will have regretted going to college.

The whole idea behind this book isn't to convince *why* you should go to college, but more *how you can afford* to go to college. I believe that in picking up this book, you've already confirmed that you believe college is worthwhile. This chapter was designed just to solidify that idea in your mind. And to show you that, on the other side, when it comes time to find a job, all of this will have been worth it.

Chapter 2

Getting Your Financial House in Order

This chapter is for the parents, who likely know that preparing to pay for college happens years before your child graduates from high school. You may have started a savings account in your child's name and started funneling money toward it. Or perhaps relatives purchased U.S. Savings Bonds that will accrue to their full value by the time the first tuition bill arrives. But even if you're late to the game, you can still feel confident that you can find a way to pay for college, as long as your financial house is in order.

So what do I mean when I say your "financial house" and getting it in order? Well, let's be honest. If you haven't been squirreling money away since day one, you're going to have to rely on future scholarships to pay for college, or you're going to have to borrow to help cover costs.

Most experts would argue that borrowing to help pay for college is a bad idea. They would argue that you should have been saving all along. But here are two problems with that sentiment.

1. You do not own a time machine. And if you *haven't* been able to save money at a rate that would have college fully covered in a 529 college savings plan, you can't go back and change the past. So you need to look to what you can do *now* and into the future to pay for college.

2. Someone once said to me, "You can borrow to pay for college, but you can't borrow to pay for retirement." So if you are committed to helping your child pay for college, you should continue to save for retirement and, if necessary, take out loans to pay for college.

Of course, I don't want you to borrow so much that you put yourself in financial ruin. In fact, I expect that your child should be borrowing money, if necessary, to pay for college as well. Nearly 35 percent of undergraduate students take out federal loans to cover tuition.[1] More about how that works—and how that won't necessarily leave your student broke—in Chapter 8: Scholarships, Grants, and Loans, Oh My!

But back to you, the parent. If none of the suggestions in this book uncover ways for you to get free money, and you're committed to sending your son or daughter to the best possible college, then you're likely going to be looking at borrowing *some* money. Surveys show that half of all parents find a way to pay for college out of current income.[2] My guess is the other half are looking at financing options, such as loans. That's why the bulk of this chapter focuses on improving your creditworthiness because, let's face it, without it, you won't be getting *any* loans.

Cleaning up your credit score

Assuming you've ever applied for a credit card, bought a car, or purchased a home, you know that your credit score is important. It can be the golden ticket to a great interest rate, or it can be a black mark on your credit history that leaves you with only high-interest loans, or, worse, not able to get loans at all.

Before I get into *how* to clean up your credit score, you need to know *what* your credit history is. There are three companies, called credit bureaus or credit reporting agencies, responsible for collecting creditworthiness information on American consumers and creating what's called our credit history. Your credit score may also be referred to as a FICO score. Those credit-reporting companies are:

- ⇨ Equifax
- ⇨ Experian
- ⇨ TransUnion

Getting your credit report

By law you can get a free credit report once every 12 months directly from each of the companies. This way you can review how banks and other financial companies see your credit history. You want to make sure that all of the information is accurate on your credit history. And you want to make sure that if there are any errors on the credit report, especially those that will reflect negatively on your creditworthiness, you get them fixed right away.

The Consumer Financial Protection Bureau (CFPB) (*www.consumerfinance.gov*) is a government agency formed in 2008 after the financial crisis. Its mission is to help Americans become smarter consumers. This increased knowledge includes dealing with and fixing your credit report.

According to the CFPB, there are a number of red flags that can show up on your credit report, which you'll need to fix right away. This includes someone else identified as you, which you would notice based on addresses where you've never lived or jobs you've never held being listed on your credit report.

Also, there might be financial errors on your credit report that you want cleared. For example, it might say that you were late in sending car payments for a Porsche when the only car you've ever owned is a Prius. And you know you paid *those* payments on time. In addition, if you've ever filed for bankruptcy, that is supposed to be dropped from your credit report after 10 years. If it's still there, you need to get it removed.

Adds the CFPB: "If you find errors, you should contact the credit reporting agency from whom you obtained the report, and the creditor or whoever provided the information (called the 'furnisher' of the information). The copy of your credit report will include information about how to dispute inaccurate or incomplete information."[3]

You should also look for any delinquencies attached to your bills. In other words, paying bills late reflects poorly on your credit history. If you do see delinquencies, you need to start working hard to pay *all* of your bills on time now. Months of on-time bill paying can make any late payments less apparent on your credit report.

If you do find that you have a credit card, for example, that you've not done a great job paying in a timely manner, do not close the credit card once you've paid off the balance. I made this error a few years ago, and learned a hard lesson from it. I covered this on my blog in a post called "Do You Know Your FICO Score?" Here's a recap of what happened.

In May 2009 we missed one credit card payment. I found this out when reviewing our credit report. Somehow I didn't see this black mark until 2016. Every other month since May 2009 to now, there was an "OK" in the box on our credit report. This "OK" indicates that we'd paid every credit card on time. So, one mistake one month in 2009 dinged us. That's because a negative "mark" on your credit history is allowed to stay there for seven years.

Another mistake is we closed that credit card soon thereafter. When you close a credit card, it can stay on your credit report for up to 10 years. So it shows up, but it's not helping you by being there. Why? When those credit reporting agencies pull your credit score, one of the things they are looking at is something called your credit utilization ratio. Basically, they want to see how much of your available credit you are currently using.

That's the biggest reason *not* to eventually get rid of that credit card. Let me explain. Let's say you have $10,000 available to you and you have a credit card balance of $8,000. You're using a greater ratio of available credit than if you had an $8,000 credit card balance with $20,000 in credit available to you. See how that works? The lower the ratio of debt to credit available, the better you look on paper.

I don't suggest that you go get more credit cards to get your utilization ratio to a better place. Opening more credit cards all at once can raise a red flag on your credit report. Rather, I'm suggesting that if you already have credit cards and are working to pay down the balance in order to increase your credit score, *do not close those credit cards when you're done paying them off.*

Learning your credit score

As far as finding out what your actual credit score is, there are some free ways to do it. You may have a credit card that provides your credit score on your monthly statement. At least one of my credit cards does this. You can also use one of those credit score companies that you see advertised on TV. Just make sure they are truly free and do not require a credit card (ironically) to sign up.

Getting a good credit score

Most Americans have a credit score between 650 and 750. Just so you know: credit scores range from the lowest of 300 to the highest of 850. An 850 is considered to be a perfect credit score. If you want to make sure you look attractive to lenders, work to get your credit score above 700, if it isn't already. If you're already in the 700s, work to get your credit score into the 800s, ideally, by paying your bills on time and optimizing your debt-utilization ratio.

Don't expect your credit score to increase immediately. You should give yourself at least a year of spotless credit behavior to see a real difference in your score. If this all seems overwhelming, I would recommend meeting with a financial expert at your bank to discuss options for dealing with your debt.

Looking at college savings plans

Most states offer what are called 529 college savings plans. These are accounts that let your money grow tax free, as long as when you eventually withdraw it, you use it for qualified educational expenses. But as you've heard me say many times already, unless you're independently wealthy and aren't expecting to receive financial aid, it is nearly impossible to save at a rate that will fully cover college in the future.

As I mentioned earlier, trying to start a 529 college savings plan when your child is older doesn't make any sense. There is no way you can squirrel away enough money to pay for college in time, unless you happen to come into a large sum of money. That said, if you have younger children, like children in elementary school or younger, you may still have college savings options.

One of the remaining college savings plans that might make sense is the prepaid tuition program. As of this writing, 11 states still offer these. With a prepaid program you are literally prepaying your child's future college tuition, but at today's rates. Considering that tuition goes up, on

average, between 3 and 5 percent each year, prepaying tuition and not having to incur 18 years of tuition increases
can add up to significant savings. In fact, even if your child
is older, prepaying tuition even just for four or six years could
add up to real savings on tuition increases you will not have
to incur when your child eventually goes to college.

Currently, as of this book's publication, the states with
prepaid tuition programs that are still enrolling new people
are:

⇨ Alabama

⇨ Florida

⇨ Illinois

⇨ Maryland

⇨ Massachusetts

⇨ Michigan

⇨ Mississippi

⇨ Nevada

⇨ Texas

⇨ Virginia

⇨ Washington State

It's important that you understand the terms of these
programs before you decide to enroll. For example, some of
these prepaid tuition programs have a limited enrollment
period, and/or they only allow you to make contributions
to the plan at certain times of the year. You wouldn't want
to miss out on that once-a-year opportunity to get into one
of these prepaid programs.

It's also important to note that, at any time, a state's
legislature may decide *not* to continue offering a prepaid

tuition program. So as I've said many times throughout this book, the information here is current when I was writing this book. I have fact-checked each of these programs, to the best of my ability, based on the information that was available at the time.

Note: You may be aware of other states that continue to have a prepaid tuition program, such as Kentucky. However, they have closed enrollment to new families at this time or may be in the process of shutting down all together.

How the Florida Prepaid Tuition Plan worked for two families

When Charlotte Baker's son Price was born in 1993, her parents gave her son an amazing gift. They paid for his college tuition. When daughter Eva was born in 1996, they gave her the same gift. How did they pay for an infant's future college tuition? They did so through the Florida Prepaid Tuition Plan.

For about $5,600 and $8,200, they purchased the equivalent of 120 credits that would cover four years at the University of Florida, and allow Price and Eva to eventually go to college for free—18 years in the future. "It was a huge blessing that our kids didn't have to worry about tuition costs," says Charlotte.

Fast forward those 18 years and Charlotte of Jacksonville is suddenly a single parent. "The peace of mind as a single mom that I have because of Florida Prepaid cannot be overstated. My children were not in danger of not being able to go to school or take on massive student loan debt because I could not afford to send them," she says. "They have been responsible to pay for their own books and that has been good for them."

In fact, Price ended up graduating college early and is applying his remaining prepaid tuition to an MBA program at the University of North Florida. Eva is an entrepreneur, so she is taking community college classes while she builds her website (*www.teensgotcents.com*) and the conference she founded (*www.theteenpreneur.com*). "So far we have gotten over $2,500 worth of classes at no out-of-pocket costs to us," Charlotte adds. "Eva pays a $25 registration fee each semester, in addition to purchasing her books."

To be clear, the Florida Prepaid Plan doesn't cover school fees or textbooks. It also doesn't cover dorm fees, though now there is a room and board option that parents can purchase in advance as well. Not convinced of the value for this family? Consider this. For the current school year, tuition to the University of Florida costs $6,380 per year for in-state students like Price and Eva. That's more than their grandparents paid for Price's *entire* college education.

"Some parents are concerned about limiting their child to the state in which they purchase the program. That didn't concern us," Charlotte adds. "We felt like if they were smart or diligent enough to get a scholarship out of state, more power to them. If that wasn't going to be the case, then they would have a solid plan to get an education. It would have to be in Florida, but that was a whole lot better than nothing."

Things worked a little differently for Kim Livengood of Sarasota who also had purchased a Florida Prepaid Tuition

Plan for her daughter Willow. In 1998, Kim spent $9,999 to prepay 120 credit hours for Willow's future college education, plus one year of room and board. Things are different for this family because Willow decided to attend school out of state. But it wasn't like Kim had thrown her money away. Willow was able to apply credits from the tuition plan to help pay tuition at her out-of-state school.

According to the Florida Prepaid Tuition website, a student has two options when using a prepaid plan to pay for an out-of-state school.

1. The state can transfer, in one lump sum, the amount that would have been paid to a Florida public college or university to cover your tuition. Then the student or family would pay the difference.

2. The state can transfer funds on a "credit-hour" basis, each time the student registers for a new semester.[4]

When Willow decided she wanted to pursue an engineering degree at Drexel University in Philadelphia, she chose to transfer funds from the prepaid plan on a credit hour basis. "So far, Drexel has applied $15,000 worth from the prepaid program towards those credits," Kim explains, "and Willow still has 56 credit hours left to apply." So her original investment of just shy of $10,000 is likely to provide more than three times that value in helping to pay for Willow's studies at Drexel. Another reason the family could afford Drexel, Kim adds, is that "Willow received some of the highest scholarships offered by the school."

Q&A

Q: Should I sell my house and downsize before my kid goes to college, so I don't look richer on paper than I need to be?

A: From a financial aid standpoint, selling your house could be a very bad idea.

"The cash you get from selling your house has to go somewhere," advises Leslie Tayne, financial attorney in Melville, NY, and author of *Life & Debt*. "Having cash available on hand is worse than having money tied up in a real estate property as equity because then it is liquid." Having these "liquid" assets (assets that can be easily and quickly converted to cash) could end up making you ineligible for financial aid because you appear to have enough cash to pay for college.

Also, you might have to pay capital gains. Generally, you can avoid paying capital gains on a home sale if you've lived in that home full-time, as your primary residence, for at least two of the past five years. If you have any questions about capital gains, please speak with your accountant.

Chapter 3

Cutting Costs at Home

This is another chapter for the parents, focusing on cutting costs at home to free up cash for college. However, if students will be covering college, these tips can apply to them as well.

There are many money-saving measures middle-class parents can make in the months and years leading up to college so they can free up cash to cover tuition bills. For example, did you know that giving up your morning cup of coffee from the coffee shop can put $2,000 back in your annual budget? This chapter focuses on both big and small changes you can make in your everyday life that can add up to a big bunch of dough.

Reviewing credit card bills to cut expenses

When was the last time you reviewed your credit card statements? I don't mean reviewing them in order to pay your bill each month. I mean *really* looking at what you're charging each month. I'm asking because there is a good chance that there is at least one charge on your credit card bill for a subscription you signed up for or a service you bought—and for which you are being billed on a monthly basis—yet you're not using it regularly. If you're not getting value from something you're paying for each month, why are you still paying for it?

Some of the most popular services that continue to show up on credit card statements include gym memberships and subscription services (music, audiobooks, newspapers, and magazines). Maybe you continue to work out regularly and listen to audiobooks at the gym or during your commute. If so, then keeping those recurring charges on your credit card makes sense. However, this exercise of reviewing your credit card statements regularly can help you to spot services you're no longer using, and keep it top of mind to continue re-evaluating the services you are paying for on a monthly basis.

Transferring credit card balances

Here's something else you need to consider as you review your credit card statements: are you paying your bills in full each month? If not, you're being charged interest. More than one-third of all credit card customers carry a balance from month to month.[1] The average American is paying about $400 a year in interest *per credit card*. If you have multiple credit cards, this amount really adds up.

What if you're paying your credit card bills late? Well, we know from Chapter 2: Getting Your Financial House in Order, this is a terrible idea, especially if you're looking to improve your credit score. In addition to wrecking your credit score, when you pay late, you get slapped with a finance or late fee charge. Those fees are often in the neighborhood of $25, sometimes higher. Pay late every month and that's an extra $300 you're spending a year.

So what's a credit card user to do? Find a way to consolidate your credit card charges. See if you can't find a zero-percent balance transfer offer. Yes, you will pay a small fee for the transfer, but you will then have a period of time that you will not be accruing interest on your credit card balance. If you're able to do this, you must do two things in addition:

1. Stop spending altogether on the credit cards from which you've transferred the balance so that the balance stays at zero.

2. Make a concerted effort to pay off as much of the transferred amount during the interest-free time as possible. Because at some point interest will kick back in, and if you haven't made a dent in that credit card debt, you'll be no better off than when you made that zero-percent balance transfer.

Make sure you're not being overcharged for auto insurance

An easy way to reduce your spending and free up cash for college is to review your auto insurance policies, and make sure you're not paying too much. One of the best ways to do that is to shop around for auto insurance. The financial website Nerdwallet.com recently did a survey that found that the average driver could save $859 a year just from shopping around for car insurance.[2]

Another way to save money on auto insurance is to bundle your auto insurance with other insurance. You can often get a discount on all of your insurance payments when one company is handling home, auto, and even life insurance.

You can get discounts on insurance if your student gets good grades. You can read more about how those discounts work in Chapter 13: Freebies and Discounts for College Students. In fact, even high school students can use their good grades to help their parents save money on car insurance.

Here's something else to consider about your auto insurance: are you *over* insured? Having more insurance may sound like a good idea, but when it comes to cars, the older the car is, the less insurance you need. I mean, you still *need* insurance, but there are certain kinds of insurance that simply do not make sense to pay for anymore.

Most often, the insurance you do not need when you have an older car is comprehensive (protection for your car for damage not caused by an accident) and collision (protection for car accidents). The rule of thumb is this:

when the value of your car is less than the annual cost of comprehensive and/or collision plus whatever deductible you might have to pay as part of the insurance coverage, then it's time to drop that coverage. This change in coverage should lower your insurance premiums overall. Not really sure what all of this means? I would suggest making an appointment with someone at your insurance company to discuss it.

Housing, transportation, and car payments

While on the subject of making sure you're not paying too much for car insurance, let's talk about vehicles, your home, and the way you get to work. Experts agree that when it comes to a family's budget, these are the three areas where we spend the most money. So let's talk about how you may be able to optimize where you live, what you drive, and how you get to work to free up cash to pay for college.

How to minimize housing costs

In Chapter 2, I answered a question about whether or not you should downsize your home so you don't look real estate rich when the financial aid office reviews your forms. From a cash-on-hand standpoint, it's a bad idea to sell your home and pocket the profit. But if your ultimate goal is to be able to afford to pay for college, selling your home or downsizing could make sense, especially if you can significantly shrink your monthly mortgage payment and doing so won't throw your family into a massive upheaval.

If moving isn't an option, what about refinancing your mortgage? Families often refinance to take advantage of lower mortgage interest rates *and* to pull out equity (in the form of cash) to pay bills, do a home renovation, or, in some cases, pay for college. But if you're looking to spend less each month on housing, then refinancing simply to shrink your monthly mortgage payment only could add up to extra cash in your pocket.

Rethinking transportation

How do you get to your job? Do you drive, take the train, or hop on a bus? How much are you spending each month going to work? Is there a way for you to cut those transportation costs?

Have you thought about asking your boss if telecommuting is an option? I mean, it might not work in every employment situation—teachers can't teach via FaceTime, for instance. But if your job doesn't require a lot of actual face time with your colleagues and instead is primarily done online, why can't you work from home? That will definitely save you on your transportation costs.

Another way to cut these costs is to get a job closer to home. If you're spending hours and hundreds of dollars each month just getting to and from work, you're putting a lot of mileage on your car and spending a lot of money on your E-Z Pass. By working closer to home, you might be able to avoid the monthly train ticket, all those tolls, and the accelerated schedule for regular car maintenance because of the excessive wear and tear on your car.

If looking for a new job is something you would seriously consider and you live near a college or university, please turn to Chapter 5: Parents Who Get a College Job. In it I offer suggestions on how to look for employment in higher education. These kinds of jobs often come with tuition benefits, something every parent of a college student would like to have.

Cutting your car costs

We've already discussed how to save money on auto insurance, and how getting a job closer to home could save you on maintaining your car. Now let's talk seriously about how you can cut your car costs.

Perhaps the easiest way to do this is to own fewer cars. Another cost saver is foregoing getting a new car every three to five years. If you've been leasing cars, that's like throwing money away, in my opinion. Why would you pay for a car that you don't even get to keep at the end of your lease? I'd rather see you buy a used car for cash and not have a monthly car payment at all.

Top five everyday expenses you can change or cut

As I mentioned at the top of this chapter, choosing to brew your coffee at home can save you as much as $2,000 a year. It's one of those top five everyday expenses that you probably don't even think about anymore, but if you changed or cut, could really affect your bottom line.

Here are those top five everyday expenses and what they're costing you annually, based on the average cost:

1. Eating dinner out ($2,800)
2. Coffee ($2,000)
3. Shopping for clothes ($1,880)
4. Buying lunch at a restaurant ($1,820)
5. Bottled water ($1,400)

Altogether, we're talking about close to $10,000 you could be saving each year, simply by cooking at home, bringing your lunch to work, making your own coffee, drinking water from the tap, and putting your clothes shopping habit on hiatus.

Q&A

Q: Does having a lot of credit card and other debt help or hurt my child's chances of getting financial aid?

A: "If parents have a lot of consumer debt, such as owing a lot on their credit cards, it could affect a student's ability to get financial aid," says financial attorney and author Leslie Tayne. It can also negatively affect the *kind* of loans they may be able to take out to pay for your college education. "If you have a lot of credit card debt, it will hurt any kind of loan you apply for, especially if you've been delinquent paying your bills on time," says Tayne. "It could make it difficult for you to get a loan or for you to get one at a favorable rate."

That is, people with minimal or no debt are always more likely to get a loan at a lower percentage rate. So, on the flipside, people with a lot of debt will be looking at loans with higher percentage rates, if they can get a loan at all. To optimize your ability to take out loans, if necessary, Tayne suggests getting out of credit card debt through a debt resolution program, also known as a debt settlement program. According to the Federal Trade Commission, a debt settlement program can help you in the following ways:

- The program negotiates with your creditors to allow you to pay a "settlement" or lump sum to resolve your debt, even if that payment doesn't happen right away.

- It helps you set up an escrow-like savings account to which you agree to transfer a specific amount of money every month. This money will eventually go toward your debt.

- Once the amount in this account reaches the settlement amount, you'll be able to send it off to settle your debt.[3]

Chapter 4

College Credits Before Graduation

This chapter is written primarily for students, but it will be of interest to parents, too. It focuses on how earning college credits before high school graduation is smart. It's smart because it can have a two-pronged benefit when it comes to college acceptance and paying for college.

These college credits could potentially save you, the person footing the college bill, money by helping the student to graduate sooner, if that's a goal, or it can help students avoid extending their time in college if they change their major.

These college credits can also make a student's transcript appear more attractive and competitive. This added competitiveness could help a student qualify for merit financial aid—good news for both parents *and* students.

There are two typical ways that high school students earn college credits before graduation.

⇨   First, students can take accelerated classes in high school. These accelerated classes usually fall under one of two umbrellas: Advanced Placement or AP classes, or International Baccalaureate or IB classes. AP classes continue to be the more popular option across America.

⇨   Second, students can take college classes while still in high school, such as at a community college, through dual-enrollment options at their high school, or during a summer college program for high school students.

In this chapter I'll outline what you need to know as you consider taking AP or IB classes in high school, or pursuing classes through a two- or four-year college. I'll also address a critical element of trying to earn college credits before you've even graduated high school—the likelihood of those college credits counting toward your four-year degree. That's not to say that they *won't count*, but you have to understand how different colleges see AP scores, IB classes, and college credits earned in high school, and what you need to keep in mind before enrolling in them.

Taking Advanced Placement (AP) classes in high school

I'll never forget the information session at the University of Michigan, one of the first schools we visited with our older daughter Jane. The admissions counselor who was leading the session was answering parent and student questions when someone in the audience asked: "Which is better—getting an A in a regular class or a B in an AP class?" The admission counselor paused and then responded, "Getting an A in an AP class."

That sums up the double-edged sword that can be AP classes. Like their name (Advanced Placement) suggests, AP classes are accelerated. They require higher-level thinking and often move at a faster speed than regular, even honors, high school classes. As such, it is often much harder for students, even strong students, to pull all As in AP classes. It can be done, but it requires a significant amount of study time and effort.

The College Board, the same people who do the SATs, is responsible for AP classes and for administering the exams. According to the College Board website, as of when I'm writing this book, there are 36 traditional AP classes offered each year. These classes fall under six categories:

- ⮕ Arts
- ⮕ English
- ⮕ History and Social Science
- ⮕ Math and Computer Science
- ⮕ Sciences
- ⮕ World Languages and Culture[1]

Within each of these categories, there are at least two courses, and in some, many more. Within World Languages and Culture, for example, there are seven languages offered and eight courses altogether.

The financial benefit of AP classes

Though they are challenging, the extra work of AP classes can pay off. How? If you score high enough on the test at the end of the academic year, your college may offer you course credit. If your score is a little lower, but still strong, some schools might not give you credit, but they will let you enroll in an upper-level course in that subject area without having to take the introductory course.

To be honest, the test is not cheap. As of this writing, it costs $93 per test.[2] Note: if you cannot afford to pay $93 for a test, you can work with your school's guidance office to apply for a fee reduction. If you qualify, you'll save $31 on the test fee.

If, like my daughters, you take multiple tests, that amount can add up. But before you write off the test because of the fees, think about it this way: even at the cheapest two-year community college, $93 won't even get you a one-credit class. A student who scores well on an AP exam often earns three or four credits at a four-year college.

The admissions benefits of AP classes

According to admissions experts, colleges are looking for students who take the most rigorous course schedule possible. "Students always ask me which is more important—their GPA or their test score," says W.C. Vance, director of admissions at Ashland University in Ashland, Ohio. "The answer is neither." Instead, he, like other admissions officers, wants to see that a student has taken the most challenging curriculum available in that high school. In addition to making your transcript rise to the top, Vance says there are additional benefits to challenging yourself in high school. "First, if they take challenging courses, they tend to do better on standardized tests," he adds. "And second, it says that this is a student who clearly indicated not only a willingness but an aptitude for being a successful college student."

In other words, if you are applying to a competitive school with a 4.0 GPA but with no AP or honors courses, and your high school offers these courses, your transcript will raise some skeptical eyebrows. Although it is great that you have a great GPA, they will ask: how much did you challenge yourself in high school? Vance says that, ideally, he would like to see at least three AP courses on a student's transcript.

Because AP classes often mimic what you can expect in college classes, AP classes are a good way for you to test drive the rigor of college. AP courses could also spark your interest in what to study in college. Spend some time on the College Board website, in the AP Courses section, looking at the different classes. Each one actually includes a "suggested major" section.

If you are thinking of studying art in college, AP classes can help you to develop a portfolio that you might need for admission to a program. Of the three AP Studio Art classes offered, at least two require students to create a portfolio of work to be submitted to the College Board as part of the AP exam process.

Make sure to take the test

My own daughters took as many AP classes in high school as their schedule would allow. Theirs was a small high school with fewer than 500 students. Despite the school's small size, there were more than a dozen AP classes for them to choose from. Unlike some schools, theirs did not have any prerequisite requirements to take an AP class. That meant that any of their classmates could sign up to take APs. Several took them to make their transcripts look more attractive, but decided not to take the exam in May.

Although this did provide some window dressing for their transcripts, they squandered the chance at college credit by skipping the test. To figure out what level score will get you credit, search college websites for "credit for AP exam" or "AP test grade credits" to see how your top schools award credit. Most colleges and universities grant college credits for exam scores of 4 or 5 only, although a few still give credit for a 3 on an AP exam.

What those college credits get you

My own daughters each went into college earning 14 and 19 college credits based on their AP exams. For my older daughter Jane, she was able to knock out some of her general education requirements based on her AP exam scores. For example, she was required to take two science classes—one lab class and one lecture class. Because of her score on her AP Environmental Science exam, she placed out of the science lecture class. This meant that she had one course "free" for taking electives. Although the "freebie" did not save us money, it did give her some more freedom at college.

My younger daughter Annie entered college with 19 college credits—in essence making her a second-semester freshman in August of her freshman year. Because she was interested in STEM (science, technology, engineering, math), but wasn't sure which of the four areas she wanted to focus on, she started in her university's college of arts and sciences. By the middle of the first semester, she realized she wanted to switch to engineering. Engineering came with a ton of prerequisites. However, because of her scores on AP exams in statistics, calculus, and biology, she was seen as already having met those prerequisites. In fact, she was able to switch to engineering in second-semester freshman year and still be ahead of other freshmen who had started the school year in engineering. In this case, the AP credits probably did end up actually saving us money. Without them, Annie might have had to extend her time in school by at least a semester because of her decision to change majors. The greatest hidden cost of college is year five, something parents and students never think about, but should.

For some people, AP credits can save significant money. If you are looking to graduate in just three years, if you plan well and score high, you can enter college with one or two semesters of credits already under your belt. Considering that the U.S. Department of Education says that the average cost per year at a public four-year college is about $15,000 and more than twice that or about $35,000 at a private four-year college, that's a real savings.[3]

If you think you might want to eventually earn a master's degree, it might be wise to target schools that are not only generous with college credits for AP exams scores, but also offer five-year combined programs. This means that if you have enough credits, you could potentially graduate a five-year program in only four years, coming out with both a bachelor's and master's degree, and having saved a year's tuition in the process.

States that make it easier to get college credit for AP exams

Once you start researching the kinds of credit you can get for your AP scores, you'll quickly realize that many schools give credit for an exam score of 4 or 5. (AP tests are graded 1–5.) Some only grant credit for a 5.

Getting a 5 isn't easy. In fact, according to College Board data, the average score for nearly all of the tests it gives is about a 3. In 2015, the last year for which data was available, only 13.3 percent of students scored a 5 on exams. Almost 20 percent got 4s, and about 25 percent got a 3.[4]

A handful of states have stepped in to make it easier for students attending its state schools to earn college credit for AP exam scores of 3 and higher. Three states (Illinois, Texas, and Virginia) have recently passed laws on this topic, requiring state colleges and universities to award college credit if a student receives at least a 3 on an AP exam. A fourth state—Ohio—has given college credit for a 3 score at its public colleges and universities since 2009. So, if you are thinking about attending a state institution, even if you are out of state, see if that state has or is considering a similar mandate for granting college credit, especially if you have a lot of 3s on your exams.

International Baccalaureate (IB) classes in high school

The International Baccalaureate program is a curriculum offered by some high schools. This curriculum culminates in exams like the AP. Some schools that offer an IB curriculum also offer an IB diploma, which is considered by many admissions officers to be a prestigious credential.

The International Baccalaureate Organization (IBO) is based in Geneva, Switzerland, and more typically used at international and private schools than in public high schools in the United States. Still, a growing number of American high schools have IB programs, and these high schools graduate students that go on to earn college credit for their IB test scores.

Though knowledge of the IB curriculum is growing, it is still not as well known as AP. As a result, more colleges and universities grant credits for AP exam scores than they do for IB exam scores. But IB seems to be catching up.

Also, there are two levels of teaching and exams within the IB curriculum: standard level and higher level. Although many colleges accept certain test scores on standard level exams, more competitive schools may only accept higher-level exam scores.

College credits for IB exam scores

When Tracy Benedict's daughter Jordan was looking at colleges, it wasn't a priority to find schools that would give her credit for her high school's IB program and her exam scores. In fact, Benedict of Douglasville, Georgia, says that her motivation to have her daughter pursue an IB curriculum was more about having her taking challenging classes so that Jordan would be better prepared when she did eventually go to college.

That said, when looking at colleges, they definitely took note of colleges and universities that did accept IB exam scores. Jordan ended up enrolling at Purdue University in West Lafayette, Indiana. Purdue gave her 12 credits based on her IB exams scores. If she were looking for an accelerated undergraduate degree program, being up 12 credits as a freshman could have potentially allowed her to graduate a semester early, and saved her family a semester of tuition and housing. But that's not part of the plan. She'll use those extra credits to allow some flexibility in her class schedule.

Despite the good news of getting 12 credits for her IB exams, not all of her IB exams got her credit. Jordan's high school only taught standard level math. She discovered that Purdue only accepted scores from higher-level math. The Benedicts found this information on the Purdue Undergraduate Admissions page on the Purdue website. Those admissions sites at the college are a great place to find out about how schools view IB exam scores in regards to credits earned.

Merit scholarships for IB exams or diplomas

Although it's great to get college credits for IB exam scores, it's even better to discover that those exam scores could land you a merit scholarship as well. The University of Rochester in Rochester, New York, offers an International Baccalaureate Scholarship to incoming freshmen; its value ranges from $2,000 to full tuition.[5] Other schools awarding merit aid to IB graduates include Savannah College of Art and Design in Savannah, Georgia. The scholarship for IB grads ranges from $3,000 to $15,000.[6] The IBO would be a great resource for tracking down additional colleges that give money for being an IB graduate. Who knows? You may just qualify for a free ride to college, all because you did well in the IB curriculum at your high school.

Pursuing courses at colleges

Beyond AP and IB classes, most high school students earn college credits by enrolling in credit-bearing classes on their own while still in high school, perhaps as a night, weekend, or summer class, or their high school offers what's called dual enrollment. This dual enrollment comes to life through a partnership the high school has with a local college.

College classes on your own

There are a number of reasons that you might take a college class on your own.

1. You are ambitious. Courses that your high school offers might not be challenging enough. You can look to a local college or summer college program to offer a higher-level educational opportunity.

2. Your high school might count it. If you have a heavy academic load or are busy with extracurricular

activities, you could take college classes in the summer. This allows you to complete some high school required classes so you can have a lighter load during the school year. As an added bonus, those classes could end up giving you college credits for use after high school and/or give your high school transcript a competitive edge.

3. You are looking to save money or have a lighter load when you get to college. Perhaps the most popular reason for high school students to take college classes is that they want to go into their freshman year of college with as many credits as possible. They do this to save money by graduating sooner. Though it is admirable to want to save money by saving a semester or two on college tuition, it is critical that you find out ahead of time *which* of these credits will count at your eventual four-year college. (See Chapter 9: Out-of-State, Community College, and International Education Options for more on how colleges treat transferred credits.)

You also might want to go to college with a few credits under your belt so that you have a lighter academic load. If you are concerned about adjusting to the heavier college load, this could help. Also, if you need to work during the school year in order to pay for school, then a lighter course load might make life easier for you. Keep in mind that to qualify for financial aid, you typically have to have at least 12 credits a semester.

If you want to graduate on time, most schools require at least 15 credits a semester. If you go to college with a few courses under your belt, you can take 12 credits during your first few semesters and still qualify for aid, plus stay on track to graduate on time.

4. You want to test-drive a college. Many colleges offer credit-bearing summer college programs for high school students as a way to introduce those students to their college—so they might apply one day. It's a great marketing tool for them, but it could be a great way for you to earn college credit before graduating high school, and see if you like being on a certain college's campus for an extended period of time. If you enroll in the college where you took the summer courses, you don't have to worry about the credits transferring.

Even with all of the reasons to take college classes during high school, W.C. Vance of Ashland University has a word of warning, if you will, about loading your high school experience with college credits. "Don't miss out on your high school experience, meaning the other stuff that might not count toward college, such as being in plays, or involved with the band, or similar activities," he says. "If you go so headstrong on earning all this college credit, you're missing out on those other things you develop in high school, like leadership skills. Don't miss out if there is something you're passionate about, and you want to do."

Earn college credits through your high school

A number of school districts in the United States have instituted what's called dual-enrollment programs in their high school. They have partnered with a local college so that their high school students can take college classes while still in high school and, sometimes, without leaving the high school campus. In some instances when high school students receive their diploma, they also graduate with an associate's degree—yes, they get a two-year college degree along with their high school diploma. Here is how that's played out for one New York family.

Tanya Kelly is a single mother of two children living in Rochester, New York. Between her own college expenses and her son's, she is about $90,000 in debt. It's a big reason behind why she is encouraging her younger child Elisabeth to take as many college credits as possible while still in high school: so Elisabeth will spend less time in college earning her degree and, therefore, Tanya can spend less time paying for college tuition.

Lucky for this family, their school district has a program in place that makes it easier for Elisabeth to earn those credits. Currently, the district partners with Monroe Community College as well as nearby Niagara University to offer college-level classes at community college prices. For example, as a junior, Elisabeth has taken Italian through the Monroe Community College program for $218. She'll be taking another class her senior year along with AP Italian. By the time she graduates high school, says her mother, she'll have had two years of college-level

Italian, which could conceivably place her out of a language requirement.

Additionally, she is taking her math class through Niagara University. It is a statistics class, which costs $215. When the class is done, she'll have earned three college credits. If she'd traveled to Niagara University or had been a student there, she would have paid nearly $3,000 for that course. At the time Elisabeth signed up, Niagara's price per credit hour was $985.

Earning all of this college credit while in high school is part of a bigger plan. Tanya hopes that Elisabeth will have the equivalent of a year's worth of college credits by the time she graduates high school so they can shave one year of tuition off a four-year degree. They already know that both the Monroe and Niagara classes are likely to transfer at a state school only—private colleges tend to be pickier about which college credits transfer and count toward a degree. Some schools only take college credits from four-year schools. Others insist that the courses that are taught at a high school versus on the college campus do not count. If you have any concerns, talk to your desired college's admissions counselor or registrar before enrolling in these dual-enrollment classes.

"We were told at her high school's open house that a SUNY (State University of New York) school would take the credits but the University of Rochester, a private college right in town, would not," Tanya recalls. So Elisabeth's college plan includes staying in New York State and focusing on SUNY schools. The only exception will be if Elisabeth decides to follow her passion for cooking and apply to the Culinary Institute of America (CIA) in Hyde

Park, New York. According to the CIA website, it has a generous credit transfer program from accredited colleges, up to 36 credits.[7] So if Elisabeth plays her credits right, she could, in fact, go into a CIA program with a year's worth of college under her chef's hat.

Should you try to shorten college?

When most people think about the college experience, they think about four years on campus. For some families it's difficult to swing four years. So you might ask if it is worth it to try to shorten college. This is a tough question.

From a purely financial standpoint, reducing your time at college can make a lot of financial sense. However, choosing a college is often not just about the finances. It is also about the experience you are looking for. It is an important time developmentally and one of the few instances in your life where you will be able to explore your interests and discover things about yourself and the world around you. Do you want to cut that short?

Other questions you need to ask yourself: Do you want to study abroad? Are internships important to you? Do you want to be involved in the arts or athletics? Are you considering a double major? How you answer questions like these will help determine if you should try to shorten your time.

Depending on the specifics of your financial situation and what you are looking to get out of college, it might be useful for you to look for a college where your academic profile is significantly higher than the average student, meaning you are likely to qualify for significant merit aid to pay for four years. With these schools, you might be trading a bit in academic reputation for a more generous aid package. (See Chapter 10: Free College (or Practically Free) for a fuller discussion of this strategy.)

Q&A

Q: Does class rank really matter when applying to college?

A: Although class rank might be great for your ego, especially if you have a good rank, colleges are looking at it less and less. In fact, the year before my youngest graduated from high school, our school district decided that the high school guidance office would *no longer* include class rank on a student's transcript.

You'll see this change reflected in how admissions officers look at students, too, says W.C. Vance. "I'm seeing less of it. Schools are putting less emphasis on class rank and more on the standardized test score, unless the college is test-optional." What often matters greatly to Vance is a student who has shown great involvement in high school through sports, arts, or volunteering. He believes that students who don't engage in high school will be the same in college. Because they never had the experience of getting involved on their high school campus, they don't know how to make the most of their college experience. And these unmotivated students are not the kind that admissions officers like Vance want to admit to their schools. So don't be *that* student.

Chapter 5

Parents Who Get a College Job

Although much of this book is written for the student, this chapter is definitely for mom and dad. So if you're not a parent, hand the book over now, or mark this chapter as something they should read later.

So, parents, have you ever considered getting a job at a college or university? The reason I'm suggesting this is because working at a college or university often comes with tuition benefits.

Working in higher education isn't just about teaching college classes. Every college or university has departments with "regular" staff in it—meaning those that don't require an advanced degree to be employed, like college professors need to teach. These departments often parallel what you might find in the corporate world: marketing, finance, human resources, and more. If you are a parent who is out of work or on the job market, this employment option may be one that makes the most financial sense overall for the family, the student, and your budget.

Working at a college or university

According to the National Center for Education Statistics (NCES), there are nearly 7,000 colleges and universities in the United States.[1] Of this number, two-thirds are four-year schools, and the remaining one-third are two-year colleges, such as junior or community colleges.

As far as the states with the most colleges and universities—and therefore the greatest potential for employment opportunities—here are the top 10, according to the NCES.[2] The states are listed here in alphabetical order:

1. California
2. Florida
3. Georgia
4. Illinois
5. Massachusetts
6. New York
7. North Carolina
8. Ohio
9. Pennsylvania
10. Texas

Overall, colleges and universities employ nearly four million people in full-time staff or faculty positions. Though that pales in comparison to the 110 million Americans employed full-time nationwide, careers at college and universities often come with additional benefits that traditional jobs likely do not offer—those aforementioned tuition benefits. As this is a book about little-known ways to pay for college, I believe it's important for parents to consider that working at a college could be one of the best ways to pay as little as possible for your child to attend college.

Before I get into the nuances of tuition benefits, let's talk first about how one might go about getting a job at a college. This includes skills that translate from the corporate world to the college world, and where and how to look for a job in higher education.

Corporate skills you can use in a college job

Here's something you might not realize: private-sector skills and experience often easily translate to a job at a college or university. Colleges need everything from information technology experts to cafeteria workers to athletic trainers for their sports teams. Colleges like hiring people with a corporate background because of their decision-making skills.

"Corporate folks are driven by the dollar, and they can make quick decisions," says Adam Berman, a Senior Director with TayganPoint Consulting Group in Washington Crossing, Pennsylvania, who spent 15 years working in higher education. "When you're building a new dorm, at some point you have to stop thinking and start building, and you need someone who will take charge and make decisions."

In addition to quicker decision-making skills, colleges and universities value employees with good communication skills. Just think about the amount of "communication" a college requires: course descriptions, alumni magazines, college website copy, fundraising letters, and more.

Another area where colleges value corporate experience, Berman says, is the career development office. "I have hired a lot of human resource people into career development," he says. "These people knew how to develop our students' skills in a way that was more likely to attract corporate recruiters and hiring managers. Sending a graduate out into the world with a degree is one thing. But to be able to send them out with stellar interview skills, a more corporate savvy image, having had internships and co-ops, as well as other experiences that someone with a corporate background can recommend they have before graduation, well, that gives them a leg up for finding a job."

Resources for finding a job at a college or university

Although you can surely look for employment opportunities on major websites that focus on job searches, to really target the higher education niche, you would be wise to target your job search using sites that focus on the world of higher education. Three I recommend are *The Chronicle of Higher Education*, *Inside Higher Ed*, and Higher Ed Jobs.

The Chronicle of Higher Education

The Chronicle of Higher Education is a trade publication for people who work in higher education. A print and digital subscription is pricey, but the job search on *www.chronicle.com* is free. Though you may not find entry-level positions on this site, most recently I saw openings in human resources, counseling, and accounting.

Inside Higher Ed

Insider Higher Ed at *www.insidehighered.com* is another trade magazine for those who work at colleges and universities, and it, too, has a free-to-use job search tool. A recent scan of this site revealed jobs in marketing and counseling as well as plenty of administrative assistant positions.

Higher Ed Jobs

The site Higher Ed Jobs at *www.higheredjobs.com* lists many of the same positions you might see on the other two higher education job sites. What sets this site apart is the fact that it lists jobs by category, including those that do not require sitting behind a desk. Some of those categories include food services, childcare services, and police and public safety.

Other higher education job-seeking resources

Besides these three sites, nearly every major university has its own internal job search engine. So if you live within a certain radius of a college or university, start visiting those schools' job sites on a regular basis to keep abreast of any hiring opportunities.

In addition, there are search firms that specialize in hiring for higher education positions. Many primarily focus on professors, provosts, and presidents, but they'll often have jobs posted that do not require a PhD. For example, I recently searched one of these websites and found jobs in marketing and communications, information technology, and finance. None of these required an advanced degree.

You can also set up your own "Google Alerts" with the terms that apply to your skillset, location, and college or university you are targeting. This way Google can do some of the heavy lifting for you, and deliver to your inbox possible job leads whenever they are posted.

Finally, keep in touch with the people you and your spouse went to college with as a way to network about job opportunities. "One of the great sources of hiring for folks outside the field of education is a university and college's own alumni network," says Berman. "It makes sense for colleges and universities to hire one of their own alumni or the spouse of one of their alumni for a whole bunch of reasons, including that because they might feel loyal to the school, they could become potential donors." At the very least, connect with your fellow grads on social media sites such as LinkedIn, Twitter, or Facebook. You never know when information about a job opening might come through your alumni network.

Tuition benefits at a college job

When I was an undergrad at NYU, there were a number of students in my classes whose parents taught at the school. These students weren't shy about the fact that, because of their parent being a professor, they were attending NYU for free.

What I didn't know then but do now is this: at some institutions, cafeteria workers and cleaning crews as well as administrative assistants are eligible to send their children to college for free or at a steep discount. This isn't a benefit reserved only for professors.

When it comes to tuition benefits, they usually fall under one of these three categories:

1. Tuition assistance (the college provides some money to pay for your child's education, even if it's at a different college).
2. Tuition remission (meaning, no tuition paid).
3. Tuition exchange programs, sometimes called tuition reciprocity. This is usually a consortium of colleges that offer reciprocal tuition agreements. A college must have membership in a tuition exchange for its employees to take advantage of tuition discounts at other schools.

Here is how the Association of American Universities describes how this benefit applies across the employment spectrum at colleges and universities: "Employees from all occupations—faculty, administrative staff, physical plant staff, security officers, and food service workers, to name a few—may receive tuition remission either for themselves and/or their family members."[3]

That said, you usually do have to be employed full-time—meaning classified as a full-time employee, not just working full-time hours—to qualify for tuition benefits. You might hear a phrase like "benefits-eligible" as a way of describing which positions get tuition benefits and which do not.

A friend of mine took what she thought was a full-time job at a Pennsylvania college, with the hopes that her sons could attend for free. It was only when she went to human resources to "activate" this benefit that she learned she was classified as a contract or "at will" employee, not the full-time employee (with full-time benefits) that she assumed she was and the benefits she assumed she had. Had she read her HR benefits package carefully when she took the job two years earlier, she may have realized that her job did not come with the benefits she sought.

In addition to having a certain position, some higher education institutions require you to work there for at least a year or more before the tuition benefit kicks in. Some colleges require at least five years of employment before you can get tuition benefits. Other schools offer this benefit immediately.

Questions to ask about tuition benefits

Because it is so important to make sure you ask the *right* questions when speaking with human resources about job opportunities at a college or university, I've put together a suggested list of questions about tuition benefits. These are the questions you must ask before you are hired so you don't take a university job without knowing if it has those coveted tuition benefits:

⇨   Which job classifications qualify for tuition benefits?

- ⇨ Is this position eligible so my children can get tuition benefits? (Some institutions offer tuition benefits to the employee only.)

- ⇨ If my job isn't classified for tuition benefits, is there an opportunity for reclassification of the position in the future?

- ⇨ Is there a period of time I will need to be employed before benefits kick in?

- ⇨ For the tuition exchange, how many tuition slots are available each year?

- ⇨ What role does seniority play for those tuition exchange slots?

- ⇨ What are the limitations to the tuition benefits, such as number of semesters allowed?

- ⇨ Are these benefits to pay for tuition only or do they cover tuition and fees, including room and board?

- ⇨ Is there an academic eligibility requirement for the student using the tuition benefits? If so, what GPA does the student have to maintain to continue receiving tuition benefits?

Tuition benefit programs

As mentioned earlier, tuition benefits that come with a job in higher education usually fall under one of these three categories:

1. Tuition remission
2. Tuition assistance
3. Tuition exchange programs

In the following sections I'll explain exactly how tuition assistance, tuition remission, and tuition exchange programs work. This is a general overview. Of course, should you become employed at a college or university, I would strongly recommend you find out directly from your human resources or benefits department *exactly* how *your* tuition benefits work. Although the descriptions I'm offering are fairly detailed, each school may have slightly different tuition benefits to offer. So it's up to you to get the details directly from your employer.

Also, it's important to note that some schools offer *multiple* tuition benefits to employees. Boston University, for example, participates in a tuition exchange, but it also offers a tuition remission program. It's the same at Baylor University. There is a tuition discount program, tuition remission, and the option to use a tuition exchange at another college or university.

Tuition remission

Tuition remission basically means free tuition. But just because a college offers "tuition remission" to its employees, it doesn't mean it refers to it exactly as that in its benefits package. You could see tuition remission called "a tuition grant" or "tuition reduction." Regardless of how an employer refers to it, it means free tuition for employees and, in many instances, their dependents—your college kids. And if you're not sure if it means what you think it means, ask!

Tuition remission is a popular benefit that schools use to attract good employees. In fact, according to a survey conducted by the College and University Professional Association for Human Resources, 98 percent of all universities and colleges offer some version of tuition remission to their employees.[4]

Unlike tuition assistance and tuition exchange programs (described later), which often have waiting periods before employees can activate the benefit, many colleges allow tuition remission programs to become active immediately after you are hired. This is likely because the majority of tuition remission programs apply to classes taken at the college or university where a parent or guardian works. They usually do not require an outlay of cash like tuition assistance does, or the negotiating of available slots like in a tuition exchange. So you may not have to plan as far ahead about getting a job on a college campus, if it offers tuition remission, for your kid to go there for free.

Tuition assistance

The tuition assistance benefit means your employer "assists" you in paying your child's tuition. Sounds simple, right? Well, that's where the easy description ends. That's because how one college defines tuition assistance could be very different from how another college defines it. Let me explain how tuition assistance worked for one family. This is a topic I originally covered on the website Living on the Cheap.

When Laura Hefty was applying for jobs years ago, after staying home full-time with her two children, she was looking for good pay and benefits. But she was also thinking ahead. That is, at the time, her children were in elementary and middle school, and she knew she wanted a job that could help her pay for their eventual college education. She found that job as the executive assistant to the

Vice President and Secretary of Princeton University in Princeton, New Jersey. Princeton offers tuition assistance.

Years later, when her son Tim became a freshman in college, Princeton helped her to pay tuition, just as Hefty had hoped. What's interesting is that Princeton provided this assistance, even though Tim wasn't a student at Princeton. Tim was actually going to Duquesne University in Pittsburgh. Even so, Princeton provided a portion of Tim's tuition, because the tuition assistance that Princeton offers applies to *any* accredited four-year institution a dependent child might attend.

"The benefit that I receive from Princeton covers 50 percent of Tim's tuition," says Hefty. "The annual tuition grant under the Children's Educational Assistance Plan increases each year and is available to faculty and staff. It kicked in for me on my fifth year work anniversary."

Although this tuition assistance covers 50 percent of tuition costs for Hefty, it might cover less for another family, if their child attends a more expensive school. That is, each year Princeton offers a set amount it will cover of tuition or 50 percent of the tuition bill, whichever is less. The year that Tim became a freshman, the total tuition assistance from Princeton amounted to $14,450 or $7,225 per semester, which happened to be 50 percent of Duquesne's tuition that year. However, if Tim had attended a college where tuition was, say, $18,000 per year, Hefty would have still received $14,450 because that was the maximum tuition grant given that year.

Hefty's daughter recently enrolled in the University of North Carolina and Princeton is picking up 50 percent of the gross tuition tab or up to that aforementioned cap, whichever is less, just like it did for her brother. That tuition grant amount increases each year for inflation. "Based on the increases each year, I estimate that the total benefit in dollars that Princeton will have contributed to Tim's education will be $62,000," says Hefty. With her daughter entering college two years later, she estimates her tuition assistance for her second child to be around $65,000. Adds Hefty, "That would total to about $127,000 I didn't have to pay in college tuition."

Some colleges have a cap on how long this tuition assistance lasts. For example, common tuition assistance packages cover eight semesters of school. For children who finish their degree in four years at a college that runs traditional semesters, this would cover every semester. However, if your child attends a school that runs trimesters, the benefit would cover less. That's because four years of college at a school on trimesters would amount to 12 semesters of class—leaving your family four semesters short for tuition assistance.

Tuition exchange programs

There are three common tuition exchange programs in the United States. One is literally called The Tuition Exchange, and it is the program that more than 660 major college and universities use. The second is the CIC Tuition Exchange Program through the Council of Independent Colleges, a group of smaller, often religious-affiliated schools. More than 430 colleges and universities participate in the CIC Tuition Exchange. There is a third, smaller tuition exchange program called the Catholic College Cooperative Tuition Exchange. More than 70 Catholic colleges participate. Many of these schools are also in the CIC Tuition Exchange.

Basically, how a tuition exchange works is your student "exchanges" a spot at a college with another student who wants to attend the college where you work. This exchange happens via a scholarship that each student uses to attend the other school tuition free. (The number is up to $34,000—the most the scholarship can cover, as of this writing. That number increases each year.)

Though tuition exchanges sound very generous, what with the free tuition and all, many schools in tuition exchanges often limit the number of scholarships they give out each year. Additionally, in some tuition exchange programs, a college "earns" the right to cash in an exchange slot for an employee's child based on how many students other colleges have "sent" to the school where you work. In other words, if you work at a popular school that many students want to attend, you should have no problem "earning" a slot to use at another school. However, just because you've earned the right to cash in on this slot or scholarship, there is no guarantee that the school your child wants to attend elsewhere will have an open slot your child can take.

For example, my husband's employer participates in a tuition exchange. One of the colleges where my younger daughter was accepted also participates in the exchange. When my husband applied for a slot at this other school for our daughter to attend for free, that school rejected the slot. It was their right to do that.

Tuition benefits for university medical center employees

Many major universities have a medical center, hospital, medical school, or health system associated with them. What you may not realize is that because of this university connection, it is possible to secure tuition benefits without working in a traditional academic building, if you will.

Take, for example, Johns Hopkins University in Baltimore, Maryland. It's a well-known school for undergraduate and graduate studies. Johns Hopkins also has a medical arm— Johns Hopkins Hospital (JHH) and Johns Hopkins Health System Corporation (JHHSC). Not only are these medical services available in Baltimore, where the school is located, but also throughout Maryland, in Washington, D.C., and at a children's hospital in Florida. According to the Johns Hopkins human resources web page, employees at both JHH and JHHSC are eligible for tuition benefits for their children. These benefits fall under the tuition assistance umbrella, and offer to pay 50 percent of the value of Johns Hopkins' freshman undergraduate tuition. You have to have worked there for at least two continuous years to qualify.

As of this writing, Johns Hopkins' freshman undergraduate tuition was about $50,000. So tuition assistance as just described could be valued at as much as $25,000 per year.

This is just one example of how you could potentially get a job at a university-affiliated medical center, hospital, or other office, and still enjoy tuition benefits most often associated with "traditional" on-campus employment.

Q&A

Q: Should I tap into my retirement to pay for college?

A: The Internal Revenue Service (IRS) definitely allows you to take money out of a retirement account to pay for educational costs. But there are a number of financial reasons *not* to do this.

For starters, if you withdraw money from a retirement account, that money is going to count as income on your tax return. That means that your income will go *up* by however much you withdrew. As you know, you need to submit your tax returns with all of your financial aid forms. This bump in income could put you over a threshold to qualify for financial aid in the next academic year. Also, you'll need to pay income tax on that higher "income" due to your withdrawal.

Additionally, with some retirement accounts, you have to pay an additional tax—as high as 25 percent of the amount taken out—beyond the income tax you will already be paying.

Finally, if you take money out of a retirement account before you turn 59 1/2, the IRS says you must pay an additional 10 percent tax for that early withdrawal. The only exception to this rule is if you use the money for a qualified educational expense. You will need to provide the paperwork to prove you used the money on tuition, and there is no guarantee the IRS will allow this exception.

So to recap: by tapping into a retirement account to pay for college, you will automatically increase your income (and not in a good way for financial aid) *and* you will have to pay additional taxes. Only you can decide if this is worth it for your family.

Part II

All About Admissions

Chapter 6

The Cost of Applying to College

When it comes to applying to college, this is clearly a milestone that involves both the parent and the student. However, when it comes to this chapter of the book, the information is definitely written with the student in mind. So let me ask you: Have you drawn up your list of colleges and universities you hope to apply to yet? How many schools are on that list right now? If you're like most American teenagers, your list has at least five schools on it because that's the average number of schools high school seniors across the country apply to each year.

Although you might think that applying to more schools is better—and it might be in some cases, especially if your list is stacked with top-notch, competitive schools—there is a big reason *not* to apply to so many schools. It costs money to apply to college and those application fees can really add up.

Thanks to the Common Application, it's easier than ever these days for students just like you to apply to dozens of different schools, if you want to. Don't know what the Common Application, referred to as the Common App, is? You'll find the Common App online at *www.commonapp.org*. It's a website that nearly 700 colleges and universities in the United States and worldwide belong to, which allows students to go to one place online to apply to multiple colleges. According to the Common App website, each year one million students use the Common App to submit some four million college applications. The Common App "opens" its new year for applying to college on August 1 of each year.

How application fees add up

The Common App doesn't charge a fee for you to use its website. But the colleges you are applying to most likely are charging an application fee. According to Common App statistics, only 40 percent of the 700 schools on the Common App are fee-free or free to apply to. In other words, 60 percent of those 700 schools—or more than 400 colleges and universities that use the Common App—*do* charge an application fee.

When my older daughter was applying to college, she had 10 colleges on her list. That meant we were looking at

$500 to $750 spent just on application fees. That's probably more than she would have spent on books for her first semester at school.

Why such a big number? Each school she was applying to was charging between $50 and $75 for application fees. In the end she applied to just two schools—one early action (University of Michigan) and one early decision (Barnard College). That was a huge savings for us. Later in this chapter I'll explain how applying early decision or early action can help cut down on application fees.

Paying for test fees and more

One of the unexpected expenses that comes with applying to college is paying to have your test scores sent to the schools. When I say test scores, I'm talking SAT, ACT, AP, and IB test results. You can't just send *your* copy of your test results to an admissions office. It has to come from the testing service itself.

There is a way to send those scores for free. With the SAT, when you register to take the test and up to about a week after you've taken the test, you can choose up to four schools to which you would like your results sent for free. That's the upside, financially. The downside is you have no idea what your scores are going to look like and, after the fact, maybe those scores aren't the ones you want schools to see. Another downside is the fact that most high school students take the SAT for the first time in their junior year. This is a long time before you might even *know* which schools you want to apply to, let alone have your scores sent. So if you choose to wait to have the scores sent *after* you get your results, you'll pay just under $12 for *each score report that is sent to a school.* Applying to 10 schools? That's $120.

Here are the costs for sending those other test scores:

- AP: $15.
- ACT: free to up to four schools when you register for test; after test, $12 per report.
- IB: free for up to six schools; $14 per transcript after that.

Applying to test-optional colleges and universities

If you really want to avoid paying to have test scores sent to colleges, you can focus your efforts on colleges that are what's called test-optional. Test-optional is exactly what it sounds like—you have the option to send your test scores or not to send your test scores. More than 200 colleges and universities have changed their admissions standards to be test-optional or, in some cases, test-flexible.

With test-flexible admissions, what this means is you still have to send test scores, but they don't have to be your ACT or SAT scores. Instead, you can choose to send AP or IB scores. So, if avoiding paying for test fees is your modus operandi, text-flexible doesn't fit this model.

That being said, there can be a big benefit to applying to these test-optional and test-flexible schools—benefits that outweigh trying to avoid paying $12 or $15 for a test score.

Let's start with text-flexible. If you tanked your standardized tests but aced your AP tests, you can send those.

Sending those AP scores instead could give you a leg up at a more competitive, test-flexible school.

Test-optional lets your transcript speak for itself because no standardized test scores are necessary. But, here's something to consider with test-optional schools. If you have great grades *and* great standardized test scores, *send them your test scores anyway.* This may sound counterintuitive, but wait: students who want to receive merit aid usually must submit their standardized test scores, even with a test-optional admissions policy. If you think there is a good chance that you'll be well above the academic profile of most people applying to this test-optional school, sending your test scores could net you merit aid that isn't available to the students who opted out of sending their SAT or ACT scores.

How to apply to college for free

Even though many colleges and universities list an application fee on the admissions' web page, there are ways that you can avoid an application fee all together. Yes, that's right, it *is* possible to apply to college for free. In many instances the way you apply for free is by getting an application fee waiver.

Here are a handful of ways you can apply to college for free. Note: all information provided here about application fees was current and correct at the time of this writing.

Apply online

It's hard to believe that, in this day and age of everything being online, students still apply to college using a paper application and snail mail. However, not every family has access to the Internet, so having paper applications is still a must. There's another reason that paper applications still exist—sometimes colleges have a rolling admissions policy that has students applying before the Common App is available on August 1. Because these colleges do not have their own online portal for accepting applications, they need the paper. Unfortunately, paper applications nearly always come with an application fee.

Finally, sometimes colleges have what's called an instant-decision day. This usually coincides with some sort of open house at the college. If you decide to apply in person, you will find out that day whether or not you are accepted. It is easier for students to complete—and admissions offices to process—in-person applications when they're done on paper. However, this is the one instance where you likely *will not* pay an application fee for submitting a paper application. Colleges nearly always waive application fees during their instant-decision days.

Given all this, many colleges encourage their students to go paperless and will waive the fee if you apply using their online application. It becomes like a coupon code you might use when you're shopping online. And this is the route that most students *do* take. According to the 2015 State of College Admissions report from the National Association for College Admission Counseling, 94 percent of college applications were submitted online.[1]

Get your application in early to save

With most regular admission college applications due around January 1, some schools offer the incentive of no application fee when you apply before a certain date. And you don't even have to apply early action or early decision to qualify. Some of these deadlines are quite early in the fall semester—October 1, November 1, or December 1—so you need to be really organized and ready to go if you want to avoid those applications fees.

Remember: college application fees *are not refundable*. So if you change your mind or even if you don't get into the college of your choice when you've applied early, you're still out that application fee.

Examples of application fee-free colleges and universities

Some of this country's elite colleges charge hefty application fees. Stanford University, for example, charges $90 to apply. Not far behind are Duke University and Columbia University, each charging $85 for their applications. But there are plenty of other elite schools that do not charge an application fee.

Some of the colleges that waive all applications fees for everyone include Smith College in Massachusetts, Colby College in Maine, and Carleton College in Minnesota. Even some universities do not charge an application fee, including Tulane University in Louisiana and Baylor University in Texas.

Use alumni connections

Ask your parents to call up their own college or university alumni association to find out if there is any fee waiver that their children (you) could qualify for if you decide to apply to their alma mater. If you know someone who attended a school you're interested in applying to, like a high school classmate, find out if having this connection can help you apply to that college for free.

Visit the campus

Many colleges will reward you with a "get out of our application fee" for free card when you go on a tour, meet with an admissions officer, or simply check in at the admissions office during a visit. During Virginia Private College Week each July, high school students who visit at least three of the 25 participating Virginia colleges—including University of Richmond, Roanoke College, and Washington & Lee University—receive up to three application waivers. Also, try to attend an open house day on campus. Admissions office representatives will usually be there to hand out application fee waivers.

Focus on the military

In Chapter 10: Free College (or Practically Free), I talk about military colleges as one of the places you can go to college for free. Having a military connection can help you get a freebie during the college application process, too.

If there is a veteran in the family, there is a chance that a non-military school may give you an application waiver. It's their small way of saying, "Thank you for your service." Another military connection that lets you avoid an application fee is by applying to one of this country's military academies. There is no application fee at schools like the U.S. Naval Academy in Annapolis, Maryland.

Apply locally

There are times when state schools will let residents of its state apply to school for free. I already mentioned the Virginia Private College Week. Well, North Carolina has its own version. In November there is North Carolina College Application Week. During those five days, five public schools within the University of North Carolina system waive their application fees.

Sometimes just being a resident of a state gets you a free pass on your application fee. Take, for example, Tulane University in New Orleans. It no longer charges its application fee to Louisiana residents that apply for admission. Tulane is a private institution. Similarly, during the month of October, many Minnesota private and public colleges and universities do not charge Minnesota students any fee when they apply.

Attend a session at your high school

If your high school is like the school my daughters attended, then colleges and universities visit the guidance office on a regular basis throughout the year. Although this may not happen every day or every week, when a college comes to your school, it is in your best interest to attend that information session. Not only does it give you a venue to meet someone from a college you may be interested in applying to, but also the admissions counselors who meet you during one of these sessions can often give out application fee waivers.

Go to college fairs

College fairs are a great way to get information about and meet representatives from dozens of colleges, all in one place. Just like when a college visits your high school, it is entirely possible to come away from one of these fairs with at least one application fee waiver.

Pros and cons of applying early admission

The majority of high school seniors apply to college regular decision. What is regular decision? It means you submit your application by January 1, and the school lets you know by April 1 if you are accepted or not. That's not to say that students won't hear earlier. Some colleges offer what are called rolling admissions. Rolling admissions are literally decisions rolled out on a consistent basis throughout the year. In other words, the colleges don't wait until that April 1 date to send out acceptance letters. They roll them out as they make their decisions.

On the other spectrum of college acceptances are early decision (ED) and early action (EA). Both require students to get their applications in on the early side, and both promise to let students know about their acceptance on the early side as well. For example, most traditional ED and EA submission deadlines are November 1. Their notification date is usually four to six weeks later—often by December 15.

Some schools offer ED 1 and 2 or EA 1 and 2. These are just two different deadlines for applying early. The deadlines for these "second" early admission dates are usually the same as regular decision—on or about January 1—but by "committing" to applying early, the school is committing to telling you their decision early, often by February 1.

So how do ED and EA save you money? Students who apply to college using ED or EA tend to apply to fewer colleges. Therefore, they pay fewer applications fees.

That said, there are definite benefits to applying to college under one of these early plans. It could increase your chances of getting into a college that might be beyond your academic reach.

Applying early decision

The National Association for College Admission Counseling found that students who applied to college under ED increased their chances of acceptance by as much as 15 percent over those who applied regular decision.[2] Many colleges report admitting anywhere between 25 and 50 percent of their incoming freshman class during the ED round of admissions. So ED applicants potentially have access to 100 percent of the slots available. This means those who choose to apply regular decision are left competing for as little as half the slots remaining in a freshman class.

Here's some more good/bad news about ED: ED is most often considered to be a "binding" decision. That means if you are accepted to a college ED, you have to go to college there. Some colleges do not make ED binding. It's important to know ahead of time if the schools you want to apply to ED require their decision to be binding or not.

So what if it *is* a binding decision? Well, if you've applied to other colleges and you received a binding ED admission, you must withdraw your applications from all other colleges and commit to the one that accepted you. But that also means that you're done with the college admissions process. Knowing where you're going to college next year, before the fall semester is over and you're on December break, can be a huge relief.

Another con to ED is it doesn't give you the opportunity to compare financial aid offers from multiple colleges. That said, admissions offices are supposed to be ethical and offer you the same financial aid package on an ED decision as they would have with a regular decision.

Applying early action

What about EA? Early action is not considered to be binding. So you could potentially apply to multiple schools by an EA deadline, and find out earlier than your peers who've applied regular decision. EA deadlines can be as early as November 1 or as late as December 1. You hear about an EA decision, on average, between four and six weeks after you've applied.

So if EA isn't binding, what is the benefit to you and the college when you apply early? For you, the benefit is obvious, psychologically. You'll know earlier where you could potentially be going to college next year. Also, many schools give out the lion's share of their merit aid to students who apply earliest to their school. If you're relying on merit aid (versus need-based aid) to help pay for college, showing your commitment to a school via your early application could significantly benefit your bottom line.

What's the benefit to the school? Even though you're not required to attend your EA-admitted school, it does give the school a better idea of what their incoming freshman class looks like. If more students are admitted early, that's less work for the admissions office to do.

Application fee waivers for financial reasons

Not every family is as lucky as mine, in that we could have afforded to pay application fees for the 10 schools Jane was originally thinking of applying to. There are already financial safeguards in place through your guidance office to help if you can't afford certain college-related expenses. Your guidance counselor can get you a fee waiver or a fee reduction for the SAT, any AP tests you may taking, and even college application fees, if your family simply cannot afford the expense. Talk to your guidance counselor about what you need to do to qualify for this kind of financial assistance.

Q&A

Q: Why do colleges charge application fees anyway?

A: You would think with the cost of tuition, housing, and fees that colleges could "front" you the cost of applying to the school. But consider this: there are about 10 million high school students in the United States. Assuming an even number of students in grades 9–12, that's 2.5 million high school seniors. Of that, some 68 percent attend college immediately after high school—meaning that 1.7 million students are applying to college each year. If, on average, American high school students are submitting five college applications each, that's 8.5 million applications that college admissions offices have to process each year.

That's a huge amount of work for these offices to do. So the reason that colleges choose to charge application fees is to help offset the cost of processing applications—namely the staff of the admissions office, and the tools, equipment, and more that the staff needs to do its job.

Here's another reason for charging applications fees: it helps to weed out students who aren't truly interested in or serious about attending a school. If you charge a fee, then you're likely increasing the chance that the students who do submit an application may have a genuine interest in becoming part of the incoming freshman class. If you're just shopping around for schools, so to speak, there's a lower chance you'll want to spend money on an application fee.

How the FAFSA affects the number of schools you apply to

In Chapter 7: FAQ on Financial Aid, I stress the importance of completing your Free Application for Federal Student Aid (FAFSA). It is the most important financial aid form you need to submit during the fall of your senior year, right around the same time you're applying to college.

One thing you may not realize is that when you complete the FAFSA, you have to list the colleges you are applying to—or hope to apply to—so that the FAFSA folks can send each school your financial information. This way, if you get in, the admissions office at each college has all the information it needs to put together your financial aid package, assuming you're getting one.

Here's another thing you may not realize: the FAFSA, which you fill out online, only has room for you to list 10 schools. This can become a huge hassle if you plan to apply to more than 10 schools. We learned this when my daughter Annie decided to apply to 15 colleges.

Because of the space limitations on the FAFSA, she had to submit her FAFSA twice. Basically, she had to confirm that the 10 schools she'd originally listed on the FAFSA had received her information. Once they confirmed that, she had to go back into her FAFSA application online and delete the schools that had already gotten her financial details. Then she had to list a whole new slew of schools to which she wanted the FAFSA to send information.

In the end it all worked out because all the schools got the information they needed in time for admissions and financial aid decisions. But looking back I'm not sure I would have encouraged her to apply to so many schools at once. She spent a number of weeks feeling uncertain about how all of this was going to work out.

Here's something else to think about with the 10-school limit on the FAFSA. Some people believe that colleges can see the order in which you've listed schools on the FAFSA, and they take that to reflect which schools are your top choices. They're not supposed to, and there are rumors that the FAFSA is going to change how it delivers this information to financial aid offices. But until that is confirmed, you would be wise to rank your schools ahead of time and then list them in order of preference when doing the FAFSA.

Chapter 7

FAQ on Financial Aid

When you think about paying for college, you're probably thinking that financial aid will help you do that. Most families do. And many families do receive financial aid. According to the College Board, the same company that does AP tests and the SATs, two-thirds of college students receive some sort of financial aid. Nearly 60 percent of that financial aid came in the form of scholarships, and almost 40 percent was federal loans. (See Chapter 8: Scholarships, Grants, and Loans, Oh My! for more on each of these financial aid options.)

Although those numbers are surely hopeful, you need to remember that one-third of students *did not* receive financial aid. This may have happened for a number of reasons, including simply *not* applying for financial aid. That sounds crazy, but the truth is there are two common reasons families don't apply for financial aid.

1. They don't know how to apply for financial aid.
2. They think they make too much money to qualify, so why bother.

Applying for financial aid

First-time college students or parents with their first child going to college likely don't know *how* to go about getting that financial aid, or *when* they are supposed to do that. One of the biggest mistakes these families make is putting off the application and not realizing that *you have to apply for financial aid at the same time you're applying for college.* So in the fall, when you're sending in your college applications, you also need to be sending in your financial aid forms. These applications usually take three forms: FAFSA from the government, the CSS Profile from the College Board, and then, sometimes, a college's own financial aid forms.

What is the FAFSA?

FAFSA stands for the Free Application for Federal Student Aid. Notice the "federal" part in there. That's because this is the application that is administered by the U.S. Department of Education. It is the most important financial aid form you will fill out. That's because if you don't complete the FAFSA, you cannot qualify for federal loans to pay for college. Federal loans are not income-dependent—meaning you cannot earn too much to qualify for one (more about federal loans in Chapter 8). Even though income doesn't determine your ability to get federal loans, you still have to include your family's income information in your FAFSA application.

On October 1 every year, the FAFSA becomes available. As you need to apply for financial aid every year, it is important to remember this FAFSA filing date. Because some schools give out financial aid money on a first come, first served basis, missing the deadline can mean that you miss out.

You complete your FAFSA online. The FAFSA is also connected to the IRS website, via something called the IRS Data Retrieval Tool, and can automatically fill in your financial information from the previous year's income tax return. Less typing for you!

Because the information is stored online, filling that form out each year is less daunting than it sounds. Unless your family's income changes greatly, or one of your siblings starts college (this usually makes you eligible for more financial aid), you can pretty much repeat information on your FAFSA from one year to another.

How the FAFSA can help in an emergency

Besides getting federal loans, perhaps the best reason to complete your FAFSA on time each year is just in case an emergency occurs. "Surprises happen and surprises can be bad, like the loss of job," says W.C. Vance. "When a student has FAFSA filed, even if they don't accept the aid, all they have to do is touch base with the financial aid office, inform them of the change in income or the emergency situation, and they can do a quick adjustment on their aid." Vance says that a student can always file a FAFSA after the fact, but then they will have to wait for it to be processed before the college can do anything to help you out. He adds, "The financial aid office isn't able to help without your FAFSA data." So consider filing the FAFSA as financial insurance you may (or may not) need during your time in college.

The CSS Profile

The CSS Profile is another college aid form. CSS stands for College Scholarship Service. It is run by the College Board—yes, the same folks that do the SAT! Some colleges require it; others do not. It's most popular with private colleges. In general, it asks more detailed financial questions than the FAFSA. If your school requires it, you typically need to fill it out around the same time that you apply for admissions. Check with the school's financial aid office to determine if they require it and what the deadline is. Each school can have a different deadline. Like the FAFSA, you will need to complete the CSS Profile every year that you are in school.

Even families who don't think they will qualify for financial aid should fill out the CSS Profile. Like the FAFSA, colleges that require it typically won't consider providing financial assistance, even merit aid, without a CSS Profile on file.

Unlike the FAFSA, which is free to file, you will have to pay a fee to the College Board to do your CSS Profile. This is not a scam.

As of this book's writing, here are the College Board fees for the CSS Profile: you'll pay $25 to have your information sent to the first college, and then $16 for each additional school. This is per student. So if you are a twin or a multiple, each of you will pay $25 to have the information sent to that first school, and then $16 per person per school thereafter.

The year you are applying as a freshman to college, especially if you're applying to many schools, those fees can add up. If your family qualified for an SAT fee waiver, based on income, you can also apply for a CSS Profile fee waiver to avoid these fees. Talk to your guidance counselor about how to get that waiver.

Even with those fees, it really is worth it. When I filled out the CSS Profile for the 2016–2017 school year—when my daughters would be a sophomore and senior in college—yes, I had to pay $50 to cover the CSS Profile for both girls and their schools, but that $50 helped us get close to $20,000 in financial aid from *each* school. One-quarter of that aid was from the federal government, which the FAFSA covered. The rest was either scholarships or grants, all from the colleges themselves. Without doing the CSS Profile, my daughters never would have qualified for scholarships and grants.

Financial aid forms from your college or university

Schools that give out financial aid directly from the college often require additional financial aid forms. Sometimes donors give money to help students who fit into very specific categories that are not covered by the FAFSA or CSS Profile. So, though this process feels redundant, it is necessary if you want to be considered for all forms of aid.

When it comes to a school's own financial aid forms, meeting their deadlines is imperative. Don't assume they are the same as the FAFSA or the CSS Profile. Call the financial aid office and ask. You don't want to miss out on getting additional financial aid simply because you missed a deadline.

Finally, some people worry that applying for financial aid will affect their ability to get into college. Many colleges promote the fact that they are need-blind or that they have need-blind admissions. That means that they will not base an admissions decision on whether or not a student needs financial aid.

Qualifying for financial aid

The two criteria that colleges use when determining if you qualify for financial aid are need and merit. Need is exactly as it sounds—does your family *need* help paying for college because your income shows that you cannot afford it? And merit is based on grades, test scores, or how well you did in high school academics, extracurricular activities, leadership positions, or volunteering.

Although the families with the greatest need are nearly always going to qualify for financial aid, you may be surprised to learn that even middle-class families can have need. This need could be based on income or the family's situation, such as having divorced parents or many children in college at the same time.

"Need is based on the family's adjusted family income from tax returns," explains Vance. So if your parents are self-employed, you may qualify. That's because their tax returns show their income after deducting expenses for their business, which can reduce income greatly. Adds Vance: "Their adjusted gross income can be very low, showing a need."

Another way seemingly comfortable families could qualify for need-based financial aid is when they have two or more children in college at the same time. Even having your younger siblings going to a private high school could make your family eligible for financial aid. When you complete the CSS Profile, it will ask things such as if your parents are paying to send younger children to private school.

As far as merit goes, it's what colleges reward you with for being a good student. Merit has nothing to do with financial need. Many colleges will use merit aid to attract students who might not otherwise attend. (See Chapter 10: Free College (or Practically Free) on how applying to colleges below your academic profile can result in bigger merit awards.)

Though merit aid does exist, it is important to recognize that it is nearly impossible to get merit aid from the country's top-ranked colleges because everyone who goes there got great grades in high school. Almost no one is getting merit aid when nearly all of the incoming freshman class has a 4.0 GPA or got a perfect score on the SATs or ACTs. If you're counting on your good grades to get you more than just admission, you may want to target your college applications toward a school where your profile is considerably stronger than the typical student and is more likely to net you merit aid.

How to read a financial aid award letter

So now that you know how to apply for financial aid and what to expect or not to expect with regards to need- or merit-based money, your final task is to understand any financial aid offers you actually receive. Usually these offers come in the form of a financial aid letter sent either electronically or in that "fat" envelope that high school students still wait to receive in their mailbox. I'd originally written on Parade.com about how to read financial aid letters. I've expanded on that topic here.

At first read, some financial aid letters will make your heart leap, as did the one my younger daughter Annie received from a private college in upstate New York. When you crunched all the numbers, they were offering her a 60 percent discount. This meant that if she attended this college, we would be paying *less* than if we sent her to a state college.

The rosy financial glow of that offer wore off quickly when we read the fine print. The lion's share of her scholarship was merit-based. That's not surprising because Annie did well on standardized tests, and she had a really high GPA in high school. However, this merit award came with some caveats that gave us pause.

For starters, it wasn't a four-year guaranteed scholarship. Those are the kind that you are, well, guaranteed to receive throughout your four years on campus. This scholarship was an annual award only.

Next, that annual award would only renew based on how well Annie did in college. It's common for merit scholarships to have a minimum GPA that you must maintain; most land somewhere between a 3.0 and 3.5 GPA. However, the offer Annie was considering came with a much steeper GPA requirement.

Frankly, we found this to be unreasonable, and we ended up feeling like the merit offer was, in essence, a bait and switch. Sure, my daughter could go to the school at a 60 percent discount her first year, but after that, the aid was a crapshoot. Although we had complete faith in Annie's academic abilities, we didn't want to add to the pressure of her freshman year. So in Annie's case, we decided to view that award as a one-year grant and assumed that the next three years would have a smaller discount, if any at all.

It was hard turning down 60 percent. But the school was not Annie's first choice. If the scholarship was guaranteed for four years, we would have had a serious discussion about trade-offs. However, with just one year guaranteed, it made more sense for her to accept an offer from her top school, even with its smaller aid package.

The moral of this story is simple. Read financial aid letters very carefully. If there are requirements to keep your aid, do a careful self-evaluation. Can you really meet them? If there is any time in life to have a little self-doubt, this is it. You need to be prepared for your worst-case scenario. If there is any concern, ask the financial aid office what your package might look like in year two without the merit aid, and then you have to decide if it is worth the risk.

Expected family contribution

A college comes up with what it calls the "Expected Family Contribution" (EFC) based on the information you shared on the FAFSA and, in the case of some colleges, on the CSS Profile form. The EFC is the amount that the college believes you can afford to pay for college. You may quickly learn that what a college believes you can afford to pay is nowhere in line with what *you* believe you can afford to pay for college.

I know that as the parents with two children in college, it was hard to understand how colleges believed we could afford to pay what amounted to my entire annual salary. What about our mortgage, our retirement savings, and our daily living expenses? The reality is that colleges expect families to pay more than many feel they are able to. That is why maximizing aid is so important.

Loans, grants, and work study

When it comes to the financial aid letter, you may notice a number of items listed. There are likely to be loans—both federal and private—grants or scholarships, and work-study programs. It's important to note that when added up, all these elements may look like a big number. But read closer to determine which of these the college is actually guaranteeing and which it is simply suggesting you secure.

(I delve more in Chapter 8 about exactly how each of these aid options work.)

Student contribution

My husband and I always told our daughters that we would pay for their college education. I realize that is not the decision that every family makes, but it was ours. That said, we also told our daughters that we expected them to work during summers and part-time during the school year. They would use this money to pay for books, activities on campus, and anything else they wanted to buy for themselves (food out with friends, clothes, or Uber rides).

Colleges have the same expectations of students. They expect that they work and contribute to their college education. This can be both a good thing and bad thing. It's a good thing because students *should* work and learn basic money management. It's a bad thing because your financial aid letter may include the expected student contribution from summer jobs.

Sometimes this student contribution is an unrealistic number for what a student should be able to earn during the summer or the academic year. If for some reason you find this student contribution assumption to be unreasonable, you can raise the issue with the financial aid office—nicely.

"In a middle-class family, a student may work to help put themselves through school, or they may have worked in high school to save up for books and expenses. All of a sudden because you work, we assume you'll do the same amount of work and assume the same amount of income when you're in college," explains Justin G. Roy, dean of admissions at Georgian Court University in Lakewood, New Jersey. "But they may not be able to work as much because they're going to school. To fix this, you have to sit down with financial aid or at least offer to come in and speak with someone." Making an effort to meet with some- one in financial aid, versus just calling or sending an e- mail, will often get you closer to the financial aid result you want. "From every person I know in financial aid," adds Roy, "they'll tell you that sitting down with them speaks volumes. Even just saying that you would love to connect on the telephone, over Skype, or another means, shows a commitment that we take seriously."

Cost of attendance

Another element in your financial aid letter is the cost of attendance—literally, what the college believes it will cost you to attend its school. When a college provides its cost of attendance, it often includes the cost for books, lab fees, and other student services. The good news here is you can often find ways to *reduce* that number on your own, which can free up cash in your budget.

For example, all schools want to ensure their students are insured and many will include the cost of health in- surance in that cost of attendance. However, if you have private health insurance, you can usually knock at least $1,000 off the bill, just by providing proof of coverage (that is, a copy of your insurance card). Another example is if you don't have a car on campus. You want to make sure that you are not paying for a parking fee. Some schools add fees like this to all of the bills and require the student to indicate that they do not want the service. (More about how to cut costs in Chapter 13: Freebies and Discounts for College Students.)

How to negotiate your financial aid award

Most American high school students apply to about five colleges. With acceptances come financial aid awards, if you qualify. If you're lucky you'll have a few financial aid awards to consider.

Once you have a few offers in hand, it is possible to go back to your top choice school and see if they'll reconsider your financial aid based on the other offers you can present to them from other schools. If you're serious about negotiating your financial aid award, make time to visit the college financial aid office in person, or at least set up a Skype or FaceTime appointment.

"Having other offers is really helpful when you come in, and I suggest the whole family come in—parents and the student," says Roy. He explains that although it's good to bring those other offers, keep in mind that offers aren't always apples to apples. "They may be looking at an offer of $15,000 versus $12,000, but what is the net price to attend that college?" In other words, if College A offers you $15,000 off of a sticker price of $45,000, your net cost will be $30,000. If College B offers you $12,000 off of a bill of $40,000, the net cost is $28,000. This means that it is actually cheaper to attend the school that gave the smaller award because the starting price is lower.

Many financial aid officers get frustrated when students focus only on the size of the award and not the net price—what you will actually pay. Make sure you add in all required fees when you are considering your net cost. If your other offers really add up to a lower sticker price for you to attend the college you are talking to, there is a chance they will revise their offer to match or beat the net price.

Roy suggests that if you're meeting with the financial aid office at a higher-tier college, where admissions are more competitive, you need to take a different approach when attempting to negotiate your financial aid offer. Rather than demand they give you more money, he suggests, "Tell them you're looking at things from an affordability perspective and what advice can they offer you." It doesn't hurt to ask if they are aware of any resources that are out there that could help you track down extra money on your own.

Finally, if the financial aid offer is way off, based on changes in your family income, also schedule a meeting with the financial aid office. These offices make their decisions based on FAFSA and CSS Profile data. But sometimes there are circumstances that those tools simply don't show. For example, when my eldest daughter was applying for financial aid, my husband had just accepted a job in a neighboring state, near a vacation destination. We had purchased a home at the new location and were having a hard time selling our old home. The CSS profile indicated that we had two residences. This gave the financial aid officer the impression that we had purchased a vacation home instead of paying for college. However, we were in fact strapped with the liability of a house that we were struggling to sell. A short conversation with a financial aid officer followed up by a letter resulted in an increase in aid.

Meeting with financial aid and explaining your family's situation could yield a positive financial result. "Financial aid offices are allowed to make what's called a professional judgment," Roy explains. "This family circumstance has changed, and I'm making a professional judgment, even though the data suggest differently."

Siblings in college

Having siblings in college at the same time can help greatly with showing financial need. If the siblings attend college together, they might qualify for special scholarships, which I discuss in Chapter 8. But in this section I want to focus on extra forms you might have to fill out to get that extra financial aid.

Because my daughters are two years apart and would overlap being in college, we knew that our chances of getting financial aid likely would increase. What we didn't know was that we would have to fill out a *fourth* financial aid form because of this.

Each college required our other daughter's school to fill out paperwork. This included confirming their enrollment, the cost of attendance, and how much financial aid the school may have given in the past. A financial aid officer had to complete and sign this form, and then send it back to our other daughter's college financial aid office.

So if you will have children overlapping in college, understand that you may need to fill out additional paperwork with the financial aid office. Or, if the financial aid letter you received does not acknowledge this additional financial hardship of having another child in college, call and ask to meet with someone in financial aid to discuss this discrepancy. It never hurts to ask.

Need-blind admissions

If you know you will need money to pay for college, then you should target your applications to colleges that call themselves need-blind. What this means is that they promise not to take your financial need into account when considering your application. Although most schools are need-blind for domestic students, if you're unsure if a college you're interested in offers need-blind admissions, search their admissions web page or, better yet, pick up the phone to call and ask. Unless you can confirm that a school is, in fact, need-blind, that means they could potentially deny you admission because they can't afford to give you or don't want to be responsible for providing the financial aid you need.

Q&A

Q: Is it worth borrowing $200,000 to study at Harvard, or is it better to go to a second-tier school that you can graduate from without any debt?

A: Some people believe that if you get into Harvard, you make Harvard work. Having Harvard on your resume could be a game changer. No one is ever going to ask, "So why did you decide to attend Harvard?" Others think differently.

"If you're Harvard material, you'll likely get full scholarships somewhere else," explains Leslie Tayne. "You may end up at a 'sub-Ivy' school, but it could still be a fantastic school. And you could get your undergraduate degree for free. The good financial decision is to go to a lesser school for free, and then you can go to Harvard for graduate school."

Chapter 8

Scholarships, Grants, and Loans, Oh My!

When your financial aid letter arrives, you'll know not only whether or not you qualified for financial aid, but also which kind of aid you received. (See Chapter 7: FAQ on Financial Aid for how to read a financial aid letter.)

Most commonly, college students receive four kinds of financial aid from their school:

⇨ scholarships

⇨ grants

⇨ loans

⇨ work-study job

In this chapter I'll explain the difference between scholarships, grants, and the various loans that might appear on your financial aid statement. Because receiving a work-study job is completely beyond your control and is at the sole discretion of the school's financial aid office, I'll only mention it briefly to explain what it is and how it is supposed to reduce your financial burden.

This chapter also discusses federal loans as well as scholarships that you can apply for outside of your school's financial aid office. Finally, I'll explain some unusual or little-known ways to score financial aid in college, including having siblings attend college together and getting grandparents to kick in transferrable tuition grants from any volunteering they might have done.

Definition of scholarships, grants, loans, and work-study jobs

When it comes to college financial aid, scholarships and grants tend to be interchangeable, in that they both do not need to be paid back. Loans *do* have to be paid back. This repayment usually starts once you've graduated. Work-study jobs, as mentioned earlier, are at the sole discretion of your college. You must submit your FAFSA in order to be considered for *any* financial aid from your school or government agencies (local, state, and federal).

Scholarships and grants

Scholarships and grants are basically the same thing. Your financial aid statement may include a generic grant in a certain amount. Or it could include what's called a named scholarship. Usually, a named scholarship is from a school's endowment (a pool of money that people have donated to the college for a specific purpose, such as helping students). A named scholarship could be merit-based (based on your good grades), your major, or need-based. Sometimes they are linked to where you are from or a demographic group you belong to. One of the benefits of receiving a named scholarship in college, besides the money, is you can put it on your resume, which is good to know when applying for jobs or internships.

There may be some drawbacks to certain grants or scholarships. For example, some may have a GPA requirement attached to them—meaning you need to maintain a GPA to keep the money coming each year. Others might be year-to-year versus having a four-year guarantee. This is all to say: make sure you read those scholarships and grant offers carefully as you weigh them, and decide where you should attend college.

How work study works

Your financial aid statement might include an amount for a work-study job, but there is no guarantee that you'll be able to get a work-study job. So it's important not to rely on that amount to help offset the cost of college.

In addition, if you do get a work-study job, you are only allowed to earn up to the amount specified in your financial aid award. That means once you've hit this threshold, you're done with your job. So in some instances, if you're planning to work in college anyway, it might make more sense to get an off-campus college job, where your earnings would be unlimited.

Federal loans

As long as you've completed your FAFSA (remember that from Chapter 7?), you will qualify for federal loans to pay for college. You don't have to take those loans, but they are there to help. Every college student qualifies for $5,500 in federal loans during their freshman year of college. This is true regardless of how much your parents earn.

Federal loans for undergraduate students come in three forms.

⮑ Federal Perkins Loan.

⮑ Direct Subsidized: This is a federal loan given based on financial need.

⮑ Direct Unsubsidized.

If you qualify for a Federal Perkins Loan, you'll actually be borrowing money from your school. Even though this is a federal program, your school decides if you will get a Perkins Loan and for how much.

The other two types of federal loans are the Direct Subsidized Loan (based on need) and the Direct Unsubsidized Loan (not based on need). Every year that you're in school and complete the FAFSA, you can get one of these loans or a combination of the two.

The loan amount you're eligible to receive increases each year you are in college. However, the government has designed it so that no student graduates from college owing more than $31,000 from these loans. The benefits of these loans are low interest rates, the fact that you don't have to start paying them back until you graduate college, and if you decide to work in certain fields, the government may forgive all of your loan debt.

As of this writing, here is the maximum amount you're eligible for each year:

⮑ $5,500 as a freshman

⮑ $6,500 as a sophomore

⮑ $7,500 as a junior and senior

If for some reason your undergraduate studies went into a fifth year, you would be eligible for a fifth year of student loans. However, if you have already taken the max the previous four years, you'll only be able to borrow $4,000 in that fifth year so your amount doesn't go more than $31,000.

Just because you're eligible to take out this amount each year, it doesn't mean that you have to. Obviously, it would be better if you can subsidize your tuition needs with financial assistance you don't have to pay back—you know, scholarships and grants. That said, these loans are helpful to have at your disposal. Plus, I believe, that if a student has skin in the game, that student is likely to take college more seriously.

Q&A

Q: What are Parent Plus loans?

A: A Parent Plus loan is actually called a Direct Plus loan and it is specifically for parents of an undergraduate student. Unlike the other kinds of direct loans that students themselves can take out, Direct Plus loans come with many more strings attached. These include:

- ⇨ Parents must have excellent credit.
- ⇨ There are fees associated with taking out this loan.
- ⇨ Parents often have to apply separately for this loan; it doesn't always come through the college's financial aid office.
- ⇨ You can only qualify for a Direct Plus loan if, via the FAFSA, you have demonstrated your financial need.

⋄ Repayment is expected to begin as soon as the loan is disbursed to your child's school. However, you may ask for a grace period.

Direct Plus loans are government loans, but getting one is more like applying for a mortgage than a traditional loan. "Parent Plus loans can be very expensive," explains Leslie Tayne. "Parents are so anxious to get the loans to pay for college that they don't stop and realize that there are a lot of closing costs involved with these loans."

You can get more information about Direct Plus loans on the U.S. Department of Education's Financial Aid website: *www.Studentaid.ed.gov*.

How to make student debt disappear

On average, college students these days graduate with about $30,000 in debt. That's right in line with the borrowing limit the U.S. Department of Education places on its Direct Subsidized and Unsubsidized Loans. Even so, wouldn't it be nice if you could make that $30,000 in debt disappear, legally?

There is something called the Public Service Loan Forgiveness Program, and it can provide those who choose to work in public service (including for the government) or for a nonprofit organization with a 501(c)(3) status the ability to wipe out their student debt. Not surprisingly, there is a catch.

Your loans are not forgiven as soon as you graduate. In fact, you have to commit to work in the chosen field for 10 years *and* you have to make your monthly loan payments on time for 10 years. Then, after 10 years, if there is any balance left on your direct loans, you'll submit specific paperwork to have the remainder of your debt wiped out.

Though this program isn't something that can help you save money paying for college *now*, it's good to know about in case you aspire to work in government, become a public school teacher, or go into law enforcement. So by your early 30s you could be student loan debt free.

It's important to note that as this book was going to print, the Public Service Loan Forgiveness Program still existed but was on the chopping block. The new administration expressed interest in doing away with this program as part of its overhaul of student loan repayment options. I want you to know about this option, but I would hate for you to rely on it as a way to make all of your student debt disappear in the future, because the program itself may disappear.

Other forms of financial aid

Although private loans are an option for financing your college education, I am *not* going to discuss them at all. Why? Because you've turned to this book for unexpected and little-known ways to pay for college. You probably already knew about private loans. And, trust me, once you complete the FAFSA and CSS Profile, you will get on the mailing list for lots of these loans. In fact, it was through one of these mailings that we learned about a private student loan company, which is one of the methods we ended up using to pay for college. It made sense for our family. It might not make sense for yours.

If your parents are helping you to pay for college, the federal government runs a program called Parent Plus loans. There are often private loans out there with lower interest rates. However, if your parents' credit isn't the best, a Plus loan might be the answer. If your parents apply for and are rejected for a Plus loan, keep in mind that you could be eligible for additional federal student loans.

In the rest of this chapter I'm going to focus on other ways to secure grants and scholarships from places other than the government. This includes:

⮑   Targeting schools based on their scholarships.

⮑   Scholarships you can apply for on your own.

How you can target schools based on their scholarships

Chances are you have at least one reason for targeting the schools to which you will be applying. It could be majors offered, location, Greek life, or something else. Perhaps another criteria to add would be schools that offer scholarship opportunities not available at every school. In the following section, you'll learn about scholarships you can get if you attend school with a sibling, scholarships given out if a family member attended the college in the past (known as an alumni or a legacy), and transfer scholarships— because not every student starts at a four-year school as a freshman. As with other information shared in this book, details here were accurate at the time of publication.

Attending college with a sibling or family member

Are you in a family with two or more people going to college at the same time? If so, you and your siblings may want to consider attending the same school, especially if that school offers a sibling discount. This discount applies if your time at school overlaps in college with an older or younger sister or brother, or if you are a twin or a multiple.

To find out if a school offers such a discount, search the financial aid office's page for phrases such as "sibling discount," "twin discount," "family scholarship," or "family grants." In my experience, this discount takes one of two forms. You get a specific amount awarded as financial aid, such as the $2,000 Quinnipiac University will apply to each sibling's annual tuition bill via its Multiple Sibling Grant. Or you get a discount applied to the tuition bill. For example, at Gonzaga University in Spokane, Washington, its family discount provides 10 percent off the older sibling's tuition. If three children in the same family enroll, the oldest sibling's tuition is discounted 20 percent and the middle sibling's tuition is discounted 10 percent. At Sterling College in Sterling, Kansas, each twin gets 50 percent off tuition.

When Delsia Fleming was looking at colleges for her twin daughters, Brittany and Brianna, a few years ago, the Burlington, New Jersey mother learned that twins who attend the same school often receive a tuition discount. Because her daughters wanted to attend college together, she focused her search efforts on schools with these discounts.

Brittany and Brianna ended up enrolling at McDaniel College in Westminster, Maryland. The college provided a $2,000 discount to the second child's tuition bill. If Brittany and Brianna had been triplets or had a third sibling going to college with them, McDaniel would have knocked $4,000 off that third child's tuition bill. This is all part of the Family Tuition Reduction Grant, as McDaniel calls it.

If you can couple these sibling discounts or family scholarships with other financial aid, the money can really add up. Taken all together, it could make a lot of sense to attend college with your sibling.

If you and a younger sibling are a year apart in school, it also might make sense for you to take a gap year after senior year of high school so that you and your younger sibling can start college at the same time, and, with one of these family scholarships, save money together. If you are thinking of this strategy, work with your sibling to determine a short list of schools to apply to. Then, you should apply in your normal year and then defer your admissions for a year to take advantage of the discount when your sister or brother goes. Of course, read the fine print for these sibling discounts to make sure that deferring enrollment won't disqualify you from using it.

Legacy scholarships

When you're applying to college, it always helps if you can mention on your application a relative that attended the same college. This makes you what's called a legacy, and colleges love legacies. That's because legacies tend to feel more affinity for their school and may be more likely to donate to it in the future.

But in the here and now, with regards to legacies, you should look to see if any colleges that your relatives attended offer legacy or family scholarships. These are sometimes called an alumni grant.

At the University of Detroit Mercy in Michigan, if your parent attended that school or the University of Detroit or Mercy College of Detroit (the latter two schools merged in 1990 to form the University of Detroit Mercy), you are eligible to receive an alumni grant—$1,000 per year. Seton Hall University in South Orange, New Jersey, has an alumni scholarship that's worth $2,000 per year and goes even deeper into your family tree. You could apply and be awarded that scholarship if you are the child, grandchild, or sibling of a Seton Hall graduate.

Schools with transfer scholarships

Seven million students enroll in community college each year. Many of them want to continue on for a four-year degree, but chances are they don't because of finances. What these students may not realize is that some colleges offer scholarships specifically for transfer students from community colleges.

Because not every student starts a four-year college as a freshman, there are ways you can sniff out colleges with transfer scholarships. In fact, simply searching using the phrase "colleges with transfer scholarships" can uncover a number of four-year institutions that are willing to put their money where their mouth is for transfer students. Just a quick search using that phrase uncovered transfer scholarship opportunities at the University of Maryland, the University of Washington, and Kent State University in Ohio.

I also found a transfer scholarship at Rider University in Lawrenceville, New Jersey. Here's why it's worth mentioning. Based on the GPA you received in community college or at another four-year college from which you are transferring, you could earn a scholarship worth between $12,000 and $22,000 per year. Justin G. Roy adds, "We have articulation agreements with several local community colleges. These agreements guarantee merit aid, in the form of a transfer scholarships, based on the student's GPA. We publish the amounts so students know exactly what they can expect as they plan to transfer." (See Chapter 9: Out-of-State, Community College, and International Education Options for more on articulation agreements.)

Organizations that can help you get transfer scholarships

At the same time that you're searching for colleges that will award transfer scholarships, I strongly encourage you to also check out two organizations that offer financial aid to community college and/or transfer students.

The first is the Jack Kent Cooke Foundation. Although the Foundation provides scholarships for all college students, it has one called the Undergraduate Transfer Scholarship. It is specifically for students who excel at the community college level and want to go on to get their bachelor's degree at a four-year college or university. The Foundation gives out scholarships of up to $40,000 each year, for up to three years.

The next is Phi Theta Kappa, the community college honor society. If you earn Phi Theta Kappa membership while in community college, you can apply for and possibly receive up to $30,000 in scholarships.

How parents and grandparents can transfer tuition grants from AmeriCorps volunteer opportunities

Did you know that your parents or grandparents volunteer service could help pay for college? If someone in your life is over age 55, started volunteering with AmeriCorps after 2009, and has spent at least one year working in certain AmeriCorps volunteer programs, that person can transfer their educational award to help you pay for college.

Basically, people who volunteer their time with AmeriCorps earn time toward awards to help pay for education. It's like the old fashioned GI Bill that soldiers in the last century used to get degrees after the war. Called the Segal AmeriCorps Education Award, it can be used by "the child, step-child, foster-child, grandchild, or step-grandchild of the individual who is eligible to transfer the award."[1]

Applying for scholarships on your own

According to Justin G. Roy of Georgian Court University, during your senior year of high school, looking for scholarships should become your part-time job. "You need to designate hours every week to this, just like you do your activities or sports," he says. "Think about it this way: if you can spend two hours one week for a $1,000 scholarship, then you've just earned $500 an hour. I'm not sure what other kind of part-time job pays that," he adds.

Roy suggests setting up a separate e-mail account for all of your college-related communications and scholarship searching. "Everyone has a personal e-mail and a work e-mail," he says. "This is your college work e-mail so that when you are working within it, you are in work mode." A word to the wise about your e-mail address: "Don't make it something crazy, because we [admissions officers] look at them," says Roy. "Make it your name, and make it clean."

Why is taking a scholarship search as seriously as a job key? That's because millions of dollars in potential scholarship money goes unused every year. As most people don't know where to look for that money or how to apply for it, they simply don't try. Or they read the criteria for a scholarship, think they won't qualify, and don't even bother applying. Roy says you should always apply, even if you meet some—not all—of the criteria.

"A lot of scholarships are foundation-based," he explains. What that means is that they *must* give out that money each year. So if they want their scholarship recipient to have a 3.5 GPA, plus five other criteria—and you apply with a 3.3 GPA or 3.4 GPA and the five criteria—there is a very good chance you could end up with that scholarship. "There are years that simply no one applies for scholarships," Roy says, adding that when scholarships list their criteria, "they are the preferences but not the absolute requirement. If you're really close, try."

One of Roy's favorite services for finding out about scholarships is *www.Fastweb.com.* "Fastweb is a fantastic resource. With Fastweb, you put in your profile information, and what happens is every day or every other day they will e-mail you the scholarships that you're eligible for, based on your profile," says Roy, who continues to "test drive" Fastweb each year so he can feel confident in recommending it to students. "I sign up for Fastweb as a different type of student—a graduate school student, a transfer student, or a first-year student," he says. He finds that, on a regular basis, he is receiving legitimate scholarship information that is relevant to whatever kind of student he's signed up to be, adding, "It's not spam."

In the rest of this chapter, learn some secrets for finding free scholarship money. And when I say free, you should never pay for scholarship money. If someone wants to charge you to submit for a scholarship, move on. It's likely a scam.

Community and local scholarships

According to W.C. Vance, director of admissions at Ashland University, one of the biggest mistakes students and parents make is not looking for scholarship opportunities in their own backyard. "Typically, donors give money for someone that's following the exact path that they did, from a certain county, or for following a certain major," he says. Although the chances might be slim that you would come from that certain county or be interested in that specific major, you'll never know unless you investigate options.

Look for scholarship opportunities on the hyper local level, such as your town or your high school. Does the PTA, local library, or a department within your high school give out scholarships? My own daughter received a $600 scholarship from her high school's music department, simply because she was in chamber choir for four years.

After you've explored those super local opportunities, expand outward from there. Is there a scholarship just for students attending college from your county? What about your state? Is there a community foundation that provides scholarships for students in your area?

Many times these scholarships aren't huge amounts of money, but they can add up. Says Vance: "I have had numerous students say that they didn't apply for a local scholarship because it's only $1,000. How can you overlook a free $1,000 award?"

Next, check to see if students from your state qualify for specific scholarships and grants. In North Carolina, for example, there is the Robertson Scholars Leadership Program. It is for North Carolina students attending either

Duke University or the University of North Carolina-Chapel Hill. Three dozen students each year get one of these full-tuition scholarships.

In Louisiana, residents attending a state school can qualify for the TOPS program. TOPS stands for Taylor Opportunity Program for Students, and it covers a portion of tuition and other fees. There are four different levels to the TOPS program. Because this is a state-sponsored scholarship, you must file a FAFSA to apply and be considered. (Remember my advice from Chapter 7 on why *everyone* should file the FAFSA?)

Also, search for state-based college scholarships for residents, and see what you come up. You may be surprised at the free money out there for the applying and taking.

Fraternal, religious, and civic organization scholarships

Another local way to find scholarships is through fraternal, social, and religious organizations. This could be your dad's Elks Club, your Girl Scout council, or the house of worship your entire family attends.

In some instances, you or a family member must be a member of the organization; in other instances, anyone can qualify for a scholarship. If the organization has a religious affiliation, recipients likely have to be of that faith and/or pursuing a degree at a college affiliated with that religion. Some organizations that provide college scholarships include:

- Elks
- Kiwanis/Key Club

- Knights of Columbus
- Lions Club
- Masons (also known as Freemasons)
- Moose International
- Rotary International

Employer scholarships

Did you know that your part-time job could give you money for college—and I don't mean from just your earnings? Many national companies have scholarships available to employees, even the part-time ones. Additionally, the company that your parents work for could be a resource for scholarship money.

Some of the big companies that provide financial assistance to their employees and their dependents include Coca-Cola, Ford, and H&R Block. Many companies with a large regional presence are also generous with scholarship money for employees' children. So if one of your parents happens to work for one of those companies, have them check with human resources to see if any such program exists to help workers pay for college.

Foundation scholarships

Many big companies have a nonprofit arm that gives out college scholarships. Take Walmart, for example; it has the Walmart Foundation. Coca-Cola, just mentioned, has the Coca-Cola Scholars Foundation program available to the public. It is separate from the education benefits available only to Coca-Cola employees.

Also, says Justin G. Roy, you should extrapolate scholarships opportunities from the ones you find. So for example, you know about the Coca-Cola Scholars. You should be asking yourself if Pepsi, Starbucks, or another beverage company has a scholarship program, and then you should head over to Google to find out.

Speaking of Google, this tech giant has at least two different scholarships programs. (Note: it is *not* called Google Scholar; that is a search engine add-on for scholarly and academic papers. It's a good reminder to search using all kinds of variations on the word *scholarship*, such as *grant*, *foundation*, and *awards*.) Back to Google having scholarships, this should lead you to find out if other tech companies have similar scholarships. Off the top of my head, I would suggest Microsoft, Apple, and HP. You can also scan the Fortune 500 list or the top tech companies on the NASDAQ to learn the names of other companies that might have college scholarships available to students like you.

You should also look into some of the bigger, national foundations to see what kind of scholarship opportunities there might be. These would include the Bill and Melinda Gates Foundation and all those companies that you see sponsoring programs on PBS or public radio. Chances are they have some money set aside for college students.

Major-specific scholarships

My daughter Annie is studying engineering in college. So one of the ways we've gone after scholarships is by focusing on major-specific scholarships.

For example, there is an organization called the Society of Women Engineers, and they have been a treasure trove of engineering scholarship information. Because engineering falls under the term STEM (science, technology, engineering, mathematics), we have also searched for scholarships using that term as well.

Although STEM is certainly a buzzword when it comes education these days, it's not the only major area with scholarship opportunities. You can find scholarships related to other majors that lead to careers where there is a huge demand, such as education and nursing.

Are you thinking of pursuing a career in restaurant management or food service? You'll definitely want to check out the scholarship available through the National Restaurant Association. The National Restaurant Association is a trade association of the restaurant industry. Its Educational Foundation gives out undergraduate scholarships between $2,500 and $10,000.

These two examples just go to show you that, based on the industry you're interested in or school you want to attend, there are definitely opportunities to seek out scholarship opportunities on your own.

Chapter 9

Out-of-State, Community College, and International Education Options

When you envision yourself going to college, where do you see yourself studying? Did you know that sometimes going out of state—even out of the country—can help save tremendously on tuition bills? Also, sometimes starting at a community college can be a smart financial option, but don't assume so without first exploring all of your options. Finally, it's common knowledge that state colleges and universities have lower sticker prices than private ones. But did you ever stop to consider that attending a state school in another state could be a cost-effective option? This chapter outlines how to figure all of that out.

The price of state colleges
and universities

Everyone knows Penn State, technically the Pennsylvania State University. It's part of the Big 10, located in a great college town, and attracts students from all over the country. When my daughters were applying to college, we lived in Pennsylvania, and Penn State was the only state university they visited and considered. Although neither ended up going there, we quickly learned two things about state universities.

1. Financial aid packages from state colleges and universities are often less generous than private colleges. This means that after aid, some private colleges are actually cheaper to attend than state colleges. (This is why you should apply to the college of your choice without regard to the published price. It is your price after financial aid that matters.)

2. State colleges and universities in your state don't always have the cheap tuition you would expect them to have.

Regarding this second point, at the time I'm writing this book, in-state tuition for Pennsylvania students is more than $40,000. If you are an out-of-state student, add another $10,000 to that number.

Another fact our family had to consider, when my girls were looking at Penn State, was the unlikelihood of getting scholarships or grants. The Penn State website states that only 35 percent of the financial aid it gives out is university scholarships and grants. Sixty-two percent of students take out loans to pay for college. The remaining three percent pay for college through private scholarships or work study. That's not to say that all public colleges and universities are more expensive than you expect. Here are the tuition prices for three more state universities in Pennsylvania:

⇨ The University of Pittsburgh (a.k.a. Pitt)—$34,000

⇨ Temple University—$32,000

⇨ West Chester University—$26,000

However, if you wanted to attend Pitt, Temple, or West Chester as an out-of-state student, you're looking at significantly more expensive tuition.

One of the ways you can make public college or university tuition affordable, as an out-of-state student, is by applying to a school that has what's called a reciprocal agreement. This means that two or more states have agreed that, under certain circumstances, out-of-state students can pay in-state tuition at a public college or university there.

States with reciprocal in-state tuition agreements

Tuition reciprocal agreements, sometimes called reciprocity programs, vary from state to state or region to region, but one thing is consistent. These agreements offer in-state tuition to out-of-state students.

Generally, there are three general types of reciprocity programs.

1. Regional, which involves multiple surrounding states.

2. State program, involving other nearby states.

3. County or college-specific programs, usually in states that otherwise don't have any reciprocal agreements in place.

Here is how these three kinds of reciprocal agreements work.

Regional reciprocal agreements

The following four regional agreements allow residents of that region to attend college out of state, at a state institution, and pay in-state tuition.

1. Midwest Student Exchange Program

The Midwest Student Exchange Program (MSEP) covers nine states in the Midwest. They are:

✪ Illinois

✪ Indiana

✪ Kansas

✪ Michigan

✪ Minnesota

✪ Missouri

✪ Nebraska

✪ North Dakota

✪ Wisconsin

Students must follow certain instructions to be eligible for tuition reduction via the MSEP. The agreement actually says that those institutions cannot charge out-of-state students more than 150 percent of the in-state resident tuition rate. So if tuition in-state is $10,000, those out-of-state students cannot pay more than $15,000 to go to school there. There are also private colleges and universities in the MSEP. They will discount tuition 10 percent for students from participating states.

2. Western Undergraduate Exchange

The Western Undergraduate Exchange (WUE) is another regional program. It covers the following 15 states:

- Alaska
- Arizona
- California
- Colorado
- Hawaii
- Idaho
- Montana
- Nevada
- New Mexico
- North Dakota
- Oregon
- South Dakota
- Utah
- Washington
- Wyoming

The WUE allows students who live in these 15 states to go to college in the other states, but pay a reduced tuition rate. Like other regional tuition agreements, students can expect to pay 150 percent of the regular in-state tuition.

The WUE tuition reduction program applies to both two- and four-year institutions. Each college and university has the right to limit how many tuition reductions it allows each year, meaning this financial aid is first come, first serve. Be sure to have a conversation with your school's admissions or financial aid staff to make sure these reductions are available for you.

3. New England Regional Student Program

The New England Board of Higher Education offers the Regional Student Program (RSP) "Tuition Break" to residents in the six New England states. Like other regional tuition reciprocity agreements, it allows residents of one state to enjoy in-state tuition at out-of-state public colleges and universities. The RSP, however, has a catch. You will only qualify for the tuition break if you choose a major at an out-of-state public college or university which *is not offered* at a public college or university in your home state.

According to the RSP website, there are more than 800 degree programs at 82 public colleges and universities in New England that meet the RSP criteria. Here are the six states that fall under the RSP umbrella:

⇨ Connecticut

⇨ Maine

⇨ Massachusetts

⇨ New Hampshire

⇨ Rhode Island

⇨ Vermont

4. Southern Regional Education Board Academic Common Market

Don't skip over this section just because you live in a state people don't normally refer to as southern. The Southern Regional Education Board (SREB) Academic Common Market covers states you might not think would be included as being in the south, such as Delaware, Maryland, and Oklahoma.

So what is the SREB Academic Common Market? It is a consortium of more than 100 colleges and universities in 15 states that offer in-state tuition to out-of-state students looking to get a degree not offered in their home state.

Thirteen of the states offer benefits for undergraduate degrees only. They are:

- ➪ Alabama
- ➪ Arkansas
- ➪ Delaware
- ➪ Georgia
- ➪ Kentucky
- ➪ Louisiana
- ➪ Maryland
- ➪ Mississippi
- ➪ Oklahoma
- ➪ South Carolina
- ➪ Tennessee
- ➪ Virginia
- ➪ West Virginia

Two states participate only for graduate degrees. That means that its residents are limited to studying at the graduate level at the other participating states at in-state tuition rates. Conversely, residents of the other states in the SREB who want to attend college in one of these two states can only use the benefit to pursue a graduate degree. Those two graduate-level participating states are:

⇨ Florida

⇨ Texas

Neighboring state reciprocal agreements

For many years I lived on the border of Pennsylvania and New Jersey. Though neither New Jersey nor Pennsylvania has tuition reciprocal agreements that my daughters could have benefitted from, plenty of other states do. If you live near a border, I would recommend checking out the following states with these college tuition agreements in place for bordering states. In this section I've also included reciprocal agreements that are specific to a state university only.

1. New Mexico-Colorado Tuition Reciprocity

Started in 2015, this reciprocity agreement is self-explanatory. Colorado college students wishing to attend school in New Mexico—and conversely New Mexico students wanting to attend school in Colorado—will be granted in-state tuition at participating public colleges. The agreement specifies that only 500 students per state can qualify each school year. So if you're serious about getting in-state tuition through this opportunity, be one of the first to apply.

2. University of Minnesota Reciprocity Program

The University of Minnesota program is somewhat unique, in that it is one state school with its own reciprocity program. Through the University of Minnesota Reciprocity Program, residents of the following three states and one Canadian province can apply to pay in-state tuition at the one of the school's five campuses:

- ⇨ Manitoba, Canada
- ⇨ North Dakota
- ⇨ South Dakota
- ⇨ Wisconsin

3. Minnesota-Wisconsin Tuition Reciprocity

This program that covers state colleges and universities in both Wisconsin and Minnesota is much more extensive than the University of Minnesota-specific program. With the Minnesota-Wisconsin Tuition Reciprocity, students in Wisconsin can pay in-state tuition at the University of Minnesota's five campuses, one of the seven Minnesota State universities (Winona State University, Bemidji State University, among others), and 13 Minnesota community and technical colleges. Minnesota students can qualify for in-state tuition at one of the 13 University of Wisconsin campuses, including the flagship one in Madison, as well as 13 Wisconsin public colleges, and seven Wisconsin community and technical colleges.

4. University of Maine Flagship Match Program

The University of Maine wants to attract students from certain Northeast, Mid-Atlantic, Midwest, and West Coast states. So it introduced the Flagship Match Program that guarantees that students from these states who meet a certain academic criteria will pay the same in-state tuition as the flagship state university in their home state.

The following are the states and the universities whose in-state tuition the University of Maine is proposing it will match for those qualifying students:

- ⇨ California (Berkeley)
- ⇨ Connecticut (UConn)
- ⇨ Illinois (Illinois)
- ⇨ Massachusetts (UMass)
- ⇨ New Hampshire (UNH)
- ⇨ New Jersey (Rutgers)
- ⇨ Pennsylvania (Penn State)
- ⇨ Rhode Island (URI)
- ⇨ Vermont (UVM)

There is some overlap with this University of Maine program and the Regional Student Program mentioned earlier, for all students living in the six New England states. That just means that these residents are lucky enough to have two ways to save on college tuition.

5. Ohio Tuition Reciprocity

The Ohio Tuition Reciprocity program includes a specific list of schools in four neighboring states where residents can enjoy in-state tuition. Those states are:

↪ Indiana

↪ Kentucky

↪ Michigan

↪ West Virginia

Please note that this tuition program is renewed every two years during Ohio's biennial budget process. As this book was going to print, the agreement was on track to be renewed on June 30, 2017. However, as there are no guarantees, if you are an Ohio resident, I would recommend checking with any schools in Indiana, Kentucky, Michigan, or West Virginia that you might be interested in attending to see if the agreement is still in effect.

6. California-Oregon Reciprocity

California and Oregon offer a tuition reciprocity program called Califoregon. It focuses on tuition discounts at California community colleges and attendance at Southern Oregon University in Ashland, Oregon.

County or local reciprocal agreements

Living on a border town or in a border county can provide tuition benefits at a much more local level. That is, rather than tuition reciprocity that spans the entire state, there are some institutions that provide this tuition discount to residents of nearby counties. Here are two examples of such programs.

1. Youngstown State University in Ohio

Youngstown State University has a generous tuition reciprocity agreement for students living in certain counties in New York, West Virginia, and Pennsylvania. Youngstown State calls this agreement the Affordable Tuition Advantage rate. If you live in a participating county in one of the three states, you would qualify for in-state Ohio tuition at the school.

Here are the states and eligible counties where you would have to live to qualify:

New York

⬦ Chautauqua

Pennsylvania

⬦ Allegheny

⬦ Armstrong

⬦ Beaver

⬦ Butler

⬦ Clarion

⬦ Crawford

⬦ Erie

⬦ Fayette

⬦ Forest

⬦ Greene

⬦ Indiana

⬦ Jefferson

⬦ Lawrence

⬦ Mercer

⬦ Venango

⬦ Warren

⬦ Washington

  ‣ Westmoreland

West Virginia

  ‣ Brooke

  ‣ Hancock

  ‣ Marshall

  ‣ Ohio

2. University of Louisville

The University of Louisville in Kentucky has a tuition agreement in place to allow for students coming from certain Southern Indiana counties to pay in-state tuition. Those counties are:

  ‣ Clark

  ‣ Crawford

  ‣ Floyd

  ‣ Harrison

  ‣ Perry

  ‣ Scott

  ‣ Washington

If you're interested in a school located near where you live—and I've not listed it here as being part of any tuition agreements—I would suggest searching its website for the phrase "tuition reciprocity" or "tuition benefits" or "border waiver" to see if they exist. Better yet, pick up the phone and call admissions. They can answer your question right away, or at least point you to someone at the institution who can.

Tuition Benefits for District of Columbia Students

If you live in Washington, D.C., then you know you don't really have any in-state colleges or universities to attend at a discounted tuition rate. Well, you might *think* that, but it's not true.

Thanks to the DC Tuition Assistance Grant (DCTAG), you can apply to receive a discounted tuition rate at state colleges and universities in any of the 50 states, plus Guam and Puerto Rico. This discounted rate amounts to a $10,000 grant that the school will apply to the difference between in-state and out-of-state tuition. So although it's not 100 percent tuition reciprocity, it's at least some kind of savings.

DCTAG isn't just limited to public college and universities. Residents can also apply for a $2,500 per year grant for private, historically black, or two-year colleges.

Is it worth it to start your education at community college?

According to research from Teachers College at Columbia University in New York City, eight in 10 students who start college at a community college intend to transfer to a four-year college to get their bachelor's degree.[1] The American Association of Community Colleges says that more than seven million students are enrolled in community college each year, in a credit-bearing program.[2]

Of those, about three million students are attending community college full-time. The rest are part-time students. Considering that there are about 20 million college students overall in this country, clearly community college is an option for many of them.

Most students I've spoken with that are in community college made the decision to start there for one of two reasons:

1.   They didn't want to go far away from home.
2.   They wanted to save money.

If you have a good reason for staying near home, then a community college might be right for you. However, if you are doing it primarily to save money, crunch some numbers to make sure that the community college route actually will save you money through the full four years of college. I'll cover this later in this chapter.

Making sure community college saves money

When you look at the average annual tuition costs at a community college ($3,430) compared with the average annual tuition costs at a public, in-state college ($9,410), it's easy to see a savings. But there is more to saving money at community college than just enrolling.

Every admissions officer I interviewed for this book said the same thing—you need to know where you're going to end up in two years *before* you even start taking classes at community college. In other words, if your ultimate goal is to get a bachelor's or master's degree at a four-year college or university, you should map out which school you might end up transferring to before embarking on an associate's degree program at a community college. You need to do this to find out ahead of time how credits from your community college will count toward your next degree. That's because you don't know if your associate's degree or community college course load will transfer 100 percent to your eventual four-year college or university.

"Two years from now, you don't want to transfer with an associate's degree, thinking you are going into your bachelor's program with 60 credits," says Justin G. Roy of Georgian Court University, "and only 40 credits transfer." With 20 credits to make up to get you on track to graduate, you're looking at one semester or more of classes you'll have to pay for at the four-year college, which we've already established is more expensive. This means that with this added course load, you could end up paying more for college and spend longer getting your degree. Adds W.C. Vance of Ashland University, "Students are surprised that the stuff they thought was going to transfer didn't, and now they have to take courses again. So they didn't end up saving any time or money at community college."

Q&A

Q: Is it worth it to get the first two years of undergrad out of the way at a lower-priced community college and then transfer to a four-year college?

A: On paper that seems like the smart option— save on two years of college tuition by attending community college. But here's something you may not have considered.

Four-year colleges are often more generous with financial aid for students who start as a freshman, especially if you are a good student. Apply to the school you intend to transfer to before you decide to enroll at community college. When they give you your financial aid package, ask them to estimate what it would be if you transferred from a community college. Compare the total cost. The four-year college may not be as expensive as you think.

However, if you are a weaker high school student and the four-year school gives merit aid to both transfer students and freshmen, you might be better off buckling down for two years at community college, concentrating on getting good grades, and shooting to qualify for a top transfer package in the future.

School transfer policies for college credits

Every college has a transfer counselor in the admissions office. Once you have identified the four-year schools where you think you could end up after community college, get in touch with the transfer admissions counselor at those schools. You want to meet with that person to find out if the course of study you're planning to pursue at the community college will be accepted at that school two years from now. Colleges use phrases such as "articulation agreement" and "block transfer policy" when talking about the relationships they have with community colleges, and how they see credits and degrees earned from there.

Keep in mind that if you do end up speaking with a transfer admissions counselor at a four-year school, this can't be a one-time deal. Education requirements at colleges change all the time. So once you've got your plan in place, check in with that admissions counselor at the start of each semester. Adds Justin G. Roy, "Keep in contact with the schools because if their general education requirements change or major requirements change, you don't want to be stuck figuring that out two years later."

State college credit transfer policies

Some states have enacted policies that guarantee that credits transfer for college students. Most often, these policies are designed for the community college to four-year college transfer. But some cover transfers of all kinds. Because it is a state policy, it usually applies to state schools only.

For example, the Commonwealth of Massachusetts has something called the Commonwealth Commitment through its Mass Transfer program, run through the Massachusetts Department of Higher Education. It is a two-sided commitment that benefits college students. The state commits to helping you save money on college by ensuring your credits from community college transfer to a state university, as long as you remain consistent in your studies and maintain a certain GPA. And students commit to completing their four-year degree in the Massachusetts state system as opposed to transferring out of state.

Ohio has a transfer program of its own, too. Called the Articulation and Transfer Policy, it was started in 1990 to make it easier for students to transfer credits between Ohio public colleges and universities. The Ohio Department of Higher Education oversees this program.

This Ohio example is a good one for you to use as a model to investigate if your own state offers a similar program. For example, I would suggest starting with your state's Department of Higher Education. Next, you'll want to search for some of the terms that are relevant to the topic, such as:

- ⇨ articulation agreement or policy
- ⇨ transfer agreement or policy
- ⇨ block transfer policy
- ⇨ community college transfer
- ⇨ associate's degree transfer

If you're looking to learn about transfer policies at certain colleges or from one specific school to another, or if there are any state transfer policies, search on each school's website using those terms, too.

Why you should apply to a four-year college anyway

You may be wondering why, in a chapter that includes tips on community college, I'm including a section on why you should apply to a four-year college. That's because I believe that while considering community college, you should go through the exercise of applying as a freshman to a four-year college. And I believe this for one simple reason—to see what you get as far as financial aid.

Back in Chapter 7: FAQ on Financial Aid, I talked about comparing offers on financial aid. Here's what you may not realize: it is possible for you to apply to a four-year college and, with financial aid, it could end up costing close to or the same as community college. Sure, scholarships exist for transfer students, as I mentioned in Chapter 8, but tons more are out there for freshman applicants.

"In admissions, we compete more heavily for freshman, in discounted prices and offering scholarships," says W.C. Vance. Adds Justin G. Roy: "Many endowed scholarships are for freshman, more so than transfers."

All of this is to say that you shouldn't disregard the kind of financial aid you could get from a four-year college, especially if you're a good student. Schools that are looking to raise their academic profile will fall all over themselves with scholarship and grant offers to get good students to enroll. Meaning, if this describes you, it really might end up being cheaper to start at that four-year school as a freshman rather than transferring in from community college two years later.

Financial aid at community college

Even with community college tuition being so much cheaper than four-year college tuition, there are opportunities to apply for—and receive—financial aid. Yes, community colleges have money in their aid till. "If you think you'll get nothing and you still get nothing, you have lost an hour of your time," says Justin G. Roy, dean of admissions at Georgian Court University, "but you may not know what you're eligible for if you don't apply." For example, some states have tuition assistance programs just for community college students. However, you would need to complete the FAFSA to qualify. (Does this advice sound familiar from Chapter 7?) So if you've decided that community college is the path you want to take, make sure you still complete your FAFSA on time and apply for any financial aid that could be out there. You've got nothing to lose but a couple of hours of your time.

That said, it's important to realize there are limits to how much financial aid you can get from the government. So getting that kind of financial aid while you're in community college could prevent you from getting it when you transfer later on.

At this writing, you can only qualify for federal Pell Grants for a total of 12 semesters. Similarly, some state aid has limits. For example, New Jersey Tuition Aid Grants are only available for nine semesters. New York TAP grants can only be used for a total of eight semesters. The amount of the award is based on your resources and the cost of the school. You don't want to use all of your state and federal financial aid at your least expensive school.

Saving money by going to college abroad

When Ann Logue's son Drew was looking at colleges, the Chicago student knew that he didn't want to stay in the snowy, cold Midwest climate. Drew focused his college search on the West Coast. One of the schools that interested him was the University of Washington. When he realized how close Vancouver, British Columbia, was, he decided to check out the University of British Columbia (UBC). It's where Drew ended up enrolling as an international economics major, and not just because he's from a family that loves to travel and navigate new cultures.

One of the draws was the school's price tag. "With the current exchange rate, having Drew go to UBC as an international student," his mother explains, "would be less than what we would pay for him as an in-state student at the University of Illinois."

The truth is that Drew wasn't even considering attending an Illinois school. In addition to applying to—and being accepted at UBC—Drew had offers from the University of Oregon and the University of California, Santa Cruz.

According to the UBC website, the cost for a year's tuition and housing is about $46,000 Canadian. Based on the current exchange rate, that's a little more than $34,000 in U.S. dollars. Although Drew received a small amount of merit aid from both Oregon and Santa Cruz, the cost of attendance at each of those schools was significantly more. The nonresident rate at Oregon is about $49,000 and the rate at Santa Cruz is more than $62,000.

His family has enjoyed other savings that come from having Drew go to college in Canada.

"On a student visa he is required to have provincial health insurance, which costs $50 U.S. per month," his mother Ann explains. On their family health insurance plan, they were paying $300 per month to insure Drew.

"We then dropped him from our health insurance, but we did have to buy an additional travel health insurance policy for when he's in the U.S. That costs $400 for the year." So all together, the family is saving about $2,600 on annual health insurance costs. When added to the slightly lower cost of attending college in Canada, you can understand why the math added up for this family.

Of course, travel becomes a big consideration if you go to school in another country. But if you were looking at U.S. colleges that were not drivable from where you live, then flying was always going to have to be a part of your budgeting process. Only you can determine if the money you'll save going to college in another country plus the added expense of travel adds up to a budget that makes sense for your family and what they can afford to pay for college.

Here's another way that going to college overseas or across the border makes sense: if one of the parents has dual citizenship. If Ann or her husband had been born in Canada, Drew would be paying only $5,000 Canadian or about $3,500 American to attend UBC.

Free college in Europe

At some European colleges you don't even need to have had a family member born there to qualify for really cheap or even free college tuition. According to CNN, college is free *for everyone* in certain European countries.[3] Government websites for Norway, Iceland, and Germany all confirmed this free tuition status at public colleges[4] and universities in these three countries. There are likely more.

Beyond the money-saving aspect, there are other intangible benefits to attending college as an international student—primarily exposure to other people and cultures, plus the experience of getting to live in an entirely different place from where you were raised.

Chapter 10

Free College (or Practically Free)

How would you like to go to college for free? Believe it or not, some states offer students tuition-free, full-ride scholarships to attend certain state schools, if the student graduates high school with a certain GPA. Additionally, some schools are completely tuition-free or offer scholarship options that make school practically free. Plus, there are other ways you can get away with barely paying anything for your college education. Because we covered free international college options in Chapter 9: Out-of-State, Community College, and International Education Options, I'm limiting the freebies to right here in the United States.

How to uncover tuition-free opportunities

Going to college for free seems completely impossible, but there are schools that continue to be tuition-free today. In some instances, those colleges require military service in exchange for your free tuition.

Military academies

The five military academies that fall under this umbrella are:

- The United States Air Force Academy in Colorado Springs, Colorado

- The United States Coast Guard Academy in New London, Connecticut

- The United States Merchant Marine Academy in Kings Point, New York

- The United States Military Academy (Army) in West Point, New York

- The United States Naval Academy (Navy) in Annapolis, Maryland

Competition to get into these military academies is fierce, plus they come with that aforementioned military service requirement. You will have to pay some money toward expenses each year, but otherwise the academies are free. Even so, you must be seriously committed to this notion of competition and service to consider this option. If you are interested in the military but don't want to attend college at a military academy, look for Reserve Officer

Training Corps (ROTC) scholarships at the college or university you are targeting. These grants cover much of your cost, but like the military academies require service after college.

Federal work colleges

Some schools expect you to work for your education. One of those work-related colleges is Berea College in Berea, Kentucky. According to Timothy W. Jordan in the college's media relations office, Berea hasn't charged tuition for 125 years.

"Every Berea College student receives a Tuition Promise Scholarship, which means no Berea student pays for tuition," says Jordan. It's important to note that admission to Berea College *is* income-dependent, meaning that students from families with limited earnings are the ones the college admits. Although most students have family income well below middle-class status, even students from the middle class can and have attended this private liberal arts college.

"The current average annual household income (for a family of four) of Berea's students is around $29,000. Family income, family size, number of dependents in college, and various extenuating factors, are all taken into consideration for admission. As a result, family income may be as much as $50,000 to $60,000 in some cases," adds Jordan.

Berea is one of seven federally recognized work colleges. Some of the work colleges are tuition-free like Berea. Others charge significantly less tuition, which is then offset by the student's requirement to work.

Here is a list of those seven colleges:

1. Alice Lloyd College, Pippa Passes, Kentucky
2. Berea College, Berea, Kentucky
3. Blackburn College, Carlinville, Illinois
4. College of the Ozarks, Point Lookout, Missouri
5. Ecclesia College, Springdale, Arkansas
6. Sterling College, Craftsbury Common, Vermont
7. Warren Wilson College, Asheville, North Carolina

Although many college students work to help pay for college, one of these work colleges could provide a unique way for you to get a degree with minimal—if any—student debt.

Schools with full rides

When you hear the term "full ride" as it relates to tuition, you probably think of college athletes who are going to college for free in exchange for their athletic prowess. It turns out that smart kids can get a full ride at some U.S. schools. You just have to know where to look (which schools) and what those full-ride scholarship programs are called.

The truth is nearly every school offers some sort of full scholarship, but usually this is for one or two students a year. That's not helpful for the majority of students looking to reduce their college costs because so few people benefit from it.

The following list includes colleges and/or scholarship programs available at multiple schools where at least a dozen (if not more) students qualify *each year* for four years of tuition, room and board, and all fees covered by a 100 percent scholarship. The key with any scholarship is to apply early. So if you see something you like at a school you're targeting, apply as soon as the application comes online.

Robertson Scholars Leadership Program

The Robertson Scholarships Leadership Program exists at two North Carolina colleges—Duke University and the University of North Carolina-Chapel Hill. More than 30 students across the two campuses receive this full-ride scholarship each year. They are also able to take classes at *both* colleges.

Vanderbilt Ingram Scholars

No relation to me (my last name is Ingram, after all), the Vanderbilt Ingram Scholars is unique to Vanderbilt University in Nashville, Tennessee. It is reserved for students who are committed to volunteer service during college *and* pursuing a career in business. More than 40 students each year receive full rides as Vanderbilt Ingram Scholars.

Organizations that offer full rides or significant scholarships

There are scholarship programs available at multiple colleges and universities across the country, usually administered through some kind of foundation or organization. Many of them have a scholars program that provides a full ride or close to a full scholarship. I've outline two worth noting and which you'll find available on dozens of campuses nationwide.

Stamps Family Charitable Foundation

The Stamps Family Charitable Foundation started in 2006 at the two schools the founders attended—the University of Michigan and Georgia Tech. Since that time, Stamps has expanded to more than 40 colleges and universities nationwide. In addition to the two original schools, both renowned in their own right, Stamps Scholarship schools include some of the nation's top institutions, including California Institute of Technology (Caltech), Dartmouth, and William and Mary. It also includes many well-known state schools: The Ohio State, UC Berkeley, University of Wisconsin, University of Connecticut, University of Maryland, University of Oregon, and many more.

You can also qualify for a Stamps Scholarship if you apply to smaller, regional colleges, such as Elizabethtown College in Lancaster County, Pennsylvania. According to that college's website, there are currently 18 Stamps scholars on campus, each receiving full-tuition scholarship plus a $6,000 stipend.

A Stamps Scholarship is merit-based and is not based on financial need. At most schools, you do not need to submit a separate application for a Stamps Scholarship. As long as you submit an application at a partner school by a certain date, you are automatically considered for the scholarship.

Bonner Scholars

Another scholarship program available at multiple colleges nationwide is the Bonner Scholars. Bonner is a service-based program that provides financial aid to students in exchange for a commitment to serve others during their time in college.

According to the Bonner website, more than 60 colleges nationwide participate, ranging from small private colleges such as Bates and Oberlin to large universities such as Rutgers and the University of Tampa. Like the Stamps Scholarship, you apply directly to the school with the Bonner program; you may have to submit a separate application to the college's Bonner office as well. It's best to contact both the admissions office and the Bonner office at those colleges to find out their application requirements, including deadlines.

Uncovering merit scholarships

Another approach to finding schools with merit-based scholarships—those that could become full rides—is searching for names often associated with these financial aid programs. I would recommend looking on college websites for scholarships and grants with names such as "presidential scholar" or "trustee scholar." You may also want to swap "fellowship" for "scholar" in your search. Other titles used for merit scholarships include provost, founders, and dean. Additionally, look for colleges with honors programs for which you may qualify. Honors programs often come with hefty merit scholarships and grants.

State programs that offer full scholarships

There is a chance that your state may offer one or more scholarship programs that allow you to attend a school in your state for free. Some of these programs are for state schools only. Some only require that the school be in the state where you graduated from high school, meaning you could potentially secure a full scholarship through your state government for a private college. The newest full scholarship option is from New York State. Here I've highlighted some of those outstanding state programs.

Excelsior Scholarship

Introduced in April 2017, the Excelsior Scholarship is a brand-new program for New York State residents to attend public colleges and universities tuition-free. This scholarship program is for public schools in the SUNY (State University of New York) and CUNY (City University of New York) system only—both two- and four-year colleges. It's important to note both the plusses and minuses of the Excelsior Scholarship.

For starters, it's geared toward solid middle-class families. That's definitely a plus. At launch, it's for families earning $100,000 a year or less. According to New York State, there are more than 940,000 middle-class families that would meet this income requirement. This is the income benchmark for the fall of 2017, when the program starts. In 2018, the income level increases to $110,000 per year, topping out at $125,000 in 2019.

The tuition-free part sounds great (and it is), but it's also part of the minuses of the Excelsior Scholarship. Students must attend college full-time in order to qualify. That is, they must take an average of 30 credits per year; this includes credits earned during summer and winter sessions. In many cases, students attending college full-time need to live on campus. The Excelsior Scholarship does *not* cover housing. Typically, annual costs for on-campus housing—room and board—are between $10,000 and $12,000. So with this scholarship, college isn't completely free. Families are still going to have to come up with at least $40,000 over four years to cover housing.

Finally, there is another "strings attached" part of this scholarship. You *must* live and work in New York State after college for as many years as you received the scholarship. So if you qualify for the Excelsior Scholarship to cover four years of college, you have to stay in New York State for four years afterward. If you move out-of-state sooner, your scholarship goes from a grant (which does not need to be paid back) to a loan (which does need to be paid back). This requirement is already proving controversial in higher education circles. So although it was current when I wrote this book, I wouldn't be surprised if it changes or is scaled back after this book is published.

Georgia Hope Programs

The Georgia Hope Programs is actually a somewhat generic term to describe a number of scholarship programs available to Georgia high school students. Within the program is the Georgia Scholars as well as the Zell Miller Scholarship. Both offer significant money toward tuition—if not full-ride opportunities—that you can use at Georgia colleges and universities. What's remarkable is this program isn't limited to state institutions only. There are private colleges in Georgia that will also accept these scholarships.

Florida Bright Futures

Florida Bright Futures scholarship program provides a full ride to state institutions. It is a super competitive program, in that only three students per year qualify. That said, when you visit the Florida Student Scholarship and Grant Programs page on the Florida Department of Education website, you'll see that Bright Futures isn't the only financial aid program available for Florida students. There are nearly a dozen more worth investigating. Sure, not all of them cover tuition 100 percent, but as I've stressed in Chapter 8, you can secure multiple scholarships on your own that could add up to cover nearly all if not 100 percent of your college costs.

If I haven't listed a program in your state here, that doesn't mean it doesn't exist. Like in other areas of this book, I would recommend touching base with your state's department of education or higher education to find out if there are statewide scholarships you can apply for. You can always look at the scholarship programs above, and pull out key phrases to do your own Google search for your state.

National Honor Society Scholarships

Were you admitted to the National Honor Society in high school? If so, that membership could net you a five-figure scholarship in college. Some colleges will give you $10,000 or more each year just for being a member of the National Honor Society in high school.

One example of this kind of scholarship is from Washington College in Chestertown, Maryland. On its financial aid page, the college says "All National Honor Society members who are admitted to Washington College are awarded a Washington College Academic Tuition Scholarship of at least $15,000 annually for up to four years." Note: this National Honor Society Scholarship amount increases for admitted freshmen each year. So the number stated above was current and correct at the time of this book's publication.

In addition to individual colleges and universities that reward you for National Honor Society membership, the organization itself offers a scholarship program. National Honor Society NHS Scholarships range from about $2,300 to more than $20,000.

Q&A

Q: Does it make sense to apply to colleges below my academic profile?

A: One strategy to score significant merit aid to pay for college is to apply to colleges below your academic profile. In other words, if your GPA, standardized tests scores, and other details are significantly better than the typical student that attends that school, you are more likely to get a top merit package. As I've mentioned elsewhere in this book, colleges are always looking to raise their academic profile, and they will often offer merit aid to get smart students to enroll.

How do you figure out who the typical student is at any school? You can search on the college's admissions page. Look for the incoming class profile, fast facts, or something similar. This is a document or page that a college updates each year to reflect the characteristics of the incoming freshman class. You can usually glean the average GPA or SAT score from there. If you are above that threshold, there is a good chance this college will offer you merit aid if you apply and are accepted.

Full-ride scholarships for firefighters in New York State

The Firemen's Association the State of New York (FASNY) offers a tuition reimbursement program for firefighters to attend community college. It works out to a free ride through the Higher Education Learning Plan (HELP). This statewide community college tuition reimbursement program is geared toward recruiting and retaining volunteer firefighters throughout New York State.

Under FASNY HELP, any active volunteer firefighter in good standing, and who hasn't already achieved a college degree, is eligible for up to 100 percent tuition reimbursement. The reimbursement is in exchange for maintaining good grades and fulfilling service requirements in one of New York's volunteer fire companies. There is no restriction on the type of academic courses that the HELP student-volunteer can pursue, either on a full-time or part-time basis. FASNY HELP also covers online courses taken through Empire State College.

Part III

Savings While in School

Chapter 11

Living Expenses On and Off Campus

Although many experts agree that living at college provides the most robust college experience, if you're worried about money, you might be thinking about living at home. That's understandable. Room and board can often add $10,000 or more at a public university and as much as $12,000 at a private college to your cost of attendance. If this dollar figure is your budget's breaking point, there may be some ways to work around it. This will take some creative planning on your part and, frankly, some sacrifice. Only you can determine if the time and effort you'll need to put into changing how and where you live for college is worth the dollars saved.

On-campus housing options

The most common place for college students to live is in an on-campus dormitory. I believe that dorm living provides all kinds of important life experiences for students living on their own for the first time. You are learning to live with other, nonfamily members, and experiencing independence for the first time. Understanding the importance of everything from keeping a schedule to doing your own laundry is all a big part of adulting.

That being said, once you are accepted to college and need to figure out where you are going to live, you should understand the different costs associated with different on-campus living options. You should also understand the pros and cons of each, financially. Here I've outlined the most common options, and how they may affect your budget and bottom line.

Room size matters

During my freshman year in college, I was placed in a triple with two strangers. It wasn't the greatest living situation for my first semester in college, but I survived. I was lucky enough to live in the same dorm for the rest of my time living on campus. Though I never got a coveted single, I did eventually move to a double, which you can imagine is *way* better than a triple.

Here's where I was lucky, too. At that time there was one charge for all the rooms in my dorm. It didn't matter if you were in a triple, a double, or a suite with five other students, your "space" in the dorm cost the same. That's not always true at college these days. In fact, size really does matter.

The smaller the space you live in and the fewer people you live with, the more you're likely to pay for housing. Take my older daughter's college as an example. There are three room prices on her campus, based on the housing they offer. The most expensive is a single. Next is a single in a suite. And then finally there is what they call a multiple occupancy room, which could be a double or triple room, or a double or triple in a suite. The difference in price between these three options is a whopping $7,000 a year.

Although this sliding scale on housing costs isn't true on all college campuses, it is much more common than it used to be. If you're committed to living on campus in college—and I will admit that I'm biased that you *should* live on campus for lots of social reasons—you may have to make peace with the fact that living with more people is the way to pay less for your housing.

Choosing the right meal plan

You'll notice that when you're looking at costs associated with college, it always says room and board. Room, no surprise, is where you live. Board, well, that covers things such as your meal plan. Room and board are like two peas in a pod, joined at the hip, or whatever cliché you want to use about one thing that always comes with another. At college you cannot get room without paying for board.

Most colleges offer a variety of meal plans. Some cost more than others because some offer more food and dining options than others. Sadly, most freshmen have to sign up for the most expensive meal plan because that's just how things are. So looking ahead to sophomore year and beyond, choose your meal plans wisely.

For example, if you know you're a late riser and therefore will never eat breakfast in a dining hall—you go right to lunch—there is no reason to get a meal plan with three meals a day on it. Similarly, if your course load often includes evening classes that go up against the dinner hour, like the late riser, you would be wise to choose a meal plan with only two meals a day. Or if you think you'll be going home or away most weekends, it's crazy to pay for meals on weekends that you'll never be around to use. You don't want to be wasting money paying for meals you don't use.

Sometimes a college's meal plan isn't X number of meals per week, but includes something called "swipes." This means how many times you can swipe your card to get food in a given semester. In some instances, local restaurants take "swipes." This offers an option for eating off campus that doesn't waste any money from your meal plan.

Bottom line with meal plans: the fewer meals or swipes you have each semester, the less money you're going to pay for the "board" part of room and board. However, you still have to eat. So what you really need to do is crunch the numbers to see if paying for a smaller meal plan won't end up *costing* more because you have to buy more groceries or eat out more because you're hungry.

Living at a sorority or fraternity

Many colleges and universities have a robust Greek life with sororities and fraternities. On some campuses upper-classmen can live in a fraternity or sorority house. This can actually end up being a slightly cheaper option than a dorm.

For example, my younger daughter lives in her Alpha Chi Omega house. Also, because the sorority has an in-house cook, we do not have to pay for a traditional "room and board" package but we're still paying something. Why? That's because the sorority is housing her and feeding her. Altogether, the price for her to live in the sorority house is about $900 cheaper a year than it was for her to live in the dorm. That's not a huge savings, but here's where we are really saving.

When she lived in the dorm, she had to choose a "board" plan that only gave her 225 meals per semester or 13 meals per week. In the sorority house, she is getting three meals a day or 21 meals per week or 357 meals per semester. So we're paying *less*, but getting *more* for our money.

If you find Greek life attractive and your college offers the option to live in one of the houses, you may want to investigate it as a way of saving some money on your room and board.

Off-campus housing options

When thinking about off-campus housing options, you need to get your dollars into an apples-to-apples arrangement. That is, you will pay rent, utilities, parking, and more monthly. Room and board is billed on a semester basis.

With the notion that the average cost for room and board at college falls in the $10,000 to $12,000 range—and that a typical school year is eight months or so long—the average monthly "rent" for room and board in a college dorm is between $1,250 and $1,500. In some markets, such as the Bay Area, Boston, or New York City, that's definitely below market. But for the rest of the country that probably seems like a lot of money to pay. My guess is you can find a place to live for cheaper rent, and likely spend less on groceries off campus.

But wait: when you pay for room and board, you're only paying for the time you'll be living on campus. When you sign a lease for an apartment, it's usually for 12 months. That means that you're still on the hook to pay rent the month you have off after fall semester ends and the summer months after the school year ends. In addition, most leases don't include heat, electricity, water, cable, and more. You have to pay for that out of pocket. Your dorm provides this for "free," because it is included in the cost of room and board. You may also have to pay for parking at your apartment. If you live so far off campus that you have to drive to class, you may have to pay for parking on campus, too. And then there's gas.

I'm not trying to undermine the possible value of saving money by living off campus. I just want to point out that you need to think about your *annual* cost for living off campus and compare that total number to the price for room and board. If you can save money, that's great. But don't automatically assume that you can save without adding up all the relevant numbers first.

When commuting from home makes sense

Look, I'm not going to lie—$10,000 to $12,000 is a lot of money. So I understand why some students might want to think about living at home and commuting to school. You're going to save a ton of money doing this.

You definitely would not be alone in choosing to live at home and commute to school. According to the Sallie Mae "How America Pays for College 2017" report, 50 percent of college students are living at home in order to save money.[1]

Like any other decision you're going to make about your college experience, you really need to weigh all of the pros and cons. To that end, I've put together a list of the pros for living at home and commuting, and a list of the cons for living at home and commuting. These include financial, emotional, and social pros and cons.

Pros

- Saves a significant amount of money on food, housing, and laundry
- No roommate distractions
- Ability to maintain ties and friendships at home
- Easier to keep a job you already had

Cons

- You're an adult living with parents
- Limited social life
- Possible long commute

- Cost of commuting, including wear and tear on your car
- If time management isn't your thing, you may be perpetually late to class
- Could affect your ability to get financial aid

I want to address this last "con" on the list. This is a legitimate concern. You have to remember that when colleges are considering financial aid, they are looking at your *total* cost of attendance. If you take $10,000 to $12,000 out of the equation, clearly your cost of attendance will be lower. This could lead whatever algorithm the financial aid office uses to determine aid to conclude that you need less financial aid overall or maybe that you don't need any at all. Because of this, I would recommend reaching out to your college's financial aid office and presenting both scenarios. Find out for sure if it might actually be cheaper for you to live on campus after all. Because even with the added costs of room and board, your financial aid package will be greater, and therefore your out-of-pocket cost will be lower.

Q&A

Q: What is the best way to save money on college when I know I want to earn a master's degree?

A: You should seriously consider schools that offer five-year programs that end with you earning both bachelor's and master's degrees. This gives you financial value while allowing for a four-year experience. Plus, if you're able to enter as a freshman with additional credits from your AP test grades, you may be able to graduate from a five-year program in just four years. That will have saved on paying an entire year's worth of tuition, room, and board.

Chapter 12

Savings on College Supplies

Do you know what one of the biggest hidden costs for college students is once they get to campus? It's personal spending. From late night snack runs to Uber rides to and from parties, these little costs can add up to big expenses for your budget. Don't forget you have to buy the actual supplies you need for class as well. So where does that leave you? You need advice on good money habits to ensure that you can avoid frivolous spending as much as possible—to the best of your ability—when you go away to college.

This chapter focuses on ways that college students can save money before and once they get to campus, such as how using gift cards and coupons can help save money in the long run. But as the biggest chunk of your personal budget is likely to go to books and school supplies, the biggest chunk of this chapter is going to talk about where you can find the most savings in the area of school supplies.

The textbook tab

When you visit a college's website and look up the cost for tuition, there's usually a whole laundry list of other things you'll have to spend money on as a student there—textbooks, other books, and supplies being some of them. And you can't forget about these added costs when figuring out how you're going to afford to pay for college.

These "extra" numbers are nothing to sneeze at. According to the College Board (the company that administers the SATs), the national average for annual textbook spending alone at four-year public colleges is close to $1,300.

Clever college students don't need to pay nearly anything close to that number when securing books for the semester. From buying online to renting books, let me share some secrets that can help college students save money big time on their books.

Buying books online

Believe it or not, Amazon.com has a huge array of college textbooks for sale, with new prices that are better than you can find in a college store. It's no surprise that so does

Barnes & Noble online because it manages more than 600 college bookstores nationwide. Here are three tips for buying books online on the cheap.

1. Before you put any textbooks in your online shopping cart, make sure you do some comparison-shopping, simply by using Google. You plug in a book's ISBN, or if you don't have that, the book's title, and the internal "search engines" on book-selling sites will sniff out the best prices online for that book.

2. Another trick that many college students have recently discovered is buying the international version of a college textbook, rather than the American version. How do you do this? Instead of logging onto Amazon.com (the ".com" ending being the U.S.-based bookseller's website), visit Amazon.ca—the Canadian version of Amazon.com. The only differences you may notice with the "international" version are some variations in spelling, such as the Canadian spelling of "favour" for the word "favor."

3. Another option? Search for older versions of a textbook. You may save the most by buying a slightly outdated edition. Though many professors may not encourage this practice openly, the truth is that when most textbooks get updated, the new information is so marginal as not to really affect your learning in the long run. In fact, sometimes the information on the inside is exactly the same, but only the cover has changed. For example, the cover of a history textbook might be

updated to reflect current events. Another reason a textbook might have a new "edition" is because it has a digital counterpart, such as free downloads or an online portal for more information. That new textbook may come with the password or access keys. If this online update *is* required to succeed in your class, then I would recommend looking to save money in other classes and buying the most up-to-date textbook for this class after all. There is no reason to gamble your GPA just to save a few bucks.

Textbook rentals

One of the newer options for securing textbooks on a budget is renting them. This makes so much more sense than the old system: buying brand-new textbooks, using them for the semester, and then selling them back to the college bookstore for a fraction of what you'd paid for them new. With textbook rentals, you pay a one-time fee for the rental and you're good to go. My daughters have rented textbooks from both Barnes & Noble and Amazon.com. Shipping your books back at the end of the semester is always free.

Renting does not make sense if you know that you're a voracious note-taker and highlighter-user when it comes to your college textbooks. However, if you're just interested in using your textbooks as reference materials, with no in-the-margin scribbling necessary, then choosing to rent makes good financial sense.

Q&A

Q: Is it possible to borrow all of my books from the library to save money on textbooks?

A: Yes! It's a little-known fact that many college and university libraries stock nearly all the books that professors assign, from the textbooks to the novels you may be reading in an English class. The borrowing approach works best if your college library belongs to what's called a consortium—that's a fancy way of saying that your college belongs to an organization, association, or is part of a larger college system.

These college consortia often share information and resources, including their libraries. That means that if the library on your campus doesn't have the book you need, you can search for and request it from another library in that consortium. One college student I know was able to do this borrowing dance for all the books she needed for her courses, and she saved about $800 per semester. Granted, she was constantly checking out and renewing these books throughout the semester. But for her, it was worth it to spend this time to save that amount of money.

Why Amazon Prime makes sense

Do you have an Amazon Prime account yet? If not, you should definitely get one when you go off to college. Or you should ask someone in your family to get one for you.

A regular Amazon Prime membership costs $99 a year as of this writing. One of the biggest benefits is free two-day shipping on purchases—well, *most* purchases. You have to make sure that the item you're choosing to buy on Amazon actually says eligible for free shipping right on the product page. Amazon Prime also offers streaming media, including access to Amazon original programming. There are many more benefits that are too long to list here.

Amazon Prime Student

This is a version of Prime called Amazon Prime Student that is for college students only and costs less. You are only allowed to have Amazon Prime Student for four years, and you need to have an .edu e-mail, which is what you'll get when you go to college. (If you haven't already noticed, all college and university websites do not end in "dot com" but "dot edu.") The first six months of Amazon Prime Student are free, and then you'll be charged 50 percent of the regular Prime annual membership. At this writing, that would amount to $49.50. Your Prime Student membership renews each year, for a total of four years, after which it automatically switches to the regular Prime membership price.

Why does an Amazon Prime Student account make sense? Well, for the free shipping, of course, but also because you can often find great deals on textbook purchases and rentals through Amazon.com. You can even sell books and make money.

Speaking of making money, Amazon Prime Student has a referral program. For every student you refer to Prime Student who signs up, you'll get a $10 Amazon credit that you can apply when shopping on the site. There is no limit to the number of $10 Amazon credits you can earn. However, they do expire after a year.

Finally, if you've ever shopped on Amazon.com, then you know that Amazon sells much more than just books. During my daughter's freshman year at college, when she wasn't allowed to have a car on campus, Amazon.com became her shopping salvation. As she couldn't just drive to the nearest supermarket, drugstore, or Target for snacks, personal care products, or other day-to-day necessities, she ordered it all on Amazon.com. That order was then delivered to her college mailbox two days later.

How gift cards can help

If you want to save money when you get to college, start stockpiling your gift cards now. They're a great way to eat out or go shopping without guilt, and not blow your budget.

One of the ways our family saves money on getting gift cards is we use credit cards with a rewards program for free or reduced-cost gift cards. Or we'll buy gift cards at a warehouse wholesale club like Costco where you can get a discount on packs of gift cards, such as $100 in P.F. Chang's gift cards for only $75 or $50 in Steak 'n Shake gift cards for only $40. Or we'll stock up at the holidays, when some companies offer BOGO (buy one, get one free) offers on gift cards.

All of this is a way of saying: when someone asks you what you need or want for your birthday, Christmas, Chanukah, high school graduation, or any other time you might receive a gift, ask for a gift card. Start doing this when you're a senior in high school so you can stockpile gift cards that can help save you money on your spending when you finally get to college.

Keep in mind, though, that some gift cards have fine print that state if you don't use them in any 12-month period, the balance on your gift card disappears. So if you do stockpile these gift cards, don't save them for too long.

Taxes and higher education

Believe it or not, some of your educational expenses could be tax deductible. You might think that only public college education would be eligible for a government benefit. However, money you spend at *any* accredited college or university, public or private, could qualify. But accredited is the key word. You can check to see if your school makes the cut by searching the U.S. Department of Education's Office of Postsecondary Education's database.

American Opportunity Tax Credit

You can thank something called the American Opportunity Tax Credit for this potential tax benefit. As of this writing—and according to the Internal Revenue Service (IRS) website—expenses paid for tuition, certain fees, and course materials for higher education can be claimed through the tax year 2017 (or the income tax return you would file in 2018). You can use this tax credit for the first four years of a college education.

Here are some ways the American Opportunity Tax Credit could benefit your family's bottom line and potentially save you money on college expenses.

You can apply for a tax credit to get reimbursed for up to $2,500 in college expenses. These are expenses for course-related books, supplies, and equipment that you don't pay for when paying your college tuition and fees, but pay for yourself out of pocket.

Also eligible for this tax credit are student fees required as a condition of enrollment or attendance, such as the lab fees my own daughter must pay as an engineering student at her college.

The following college-related expenses do *not* qualify for a tax deduction:

 ➪ Room and board.
 ➪ Transportation.
 ➪ Insurance.
 ➪ Medical expenses.
 ➪ Student fees not related to an enrollment or attendance requirement.

Income limits

This tax credit is "income dependent." That means if your family makes too much, you can't claim this tax credit on your tax return. But the income range is quite large and squarely covers the middle class.

Here is how the IRS describes the income limits for taking tax deductions for education expenses:

> [Taxpayers] whose modified adjusted gross income is $80,000 or less ($160,000 or less for joint filers) can claim the credit for the qualified expenses of an eligible student. The credit is reduced if a taxpayer's modified adjusted gross income exceeds those amounts. A taxpayer whose modified adjusted gross income is greater than $90,000 ($180,000 for joint filers) cannot claim the credit.[1]

If your parents are thinking of claiming the American Opportunity Tax Credit on their tax return, which they can do if they claim you as a dependent, their modified adjusted gross income must fall between $80,000 (for a single parent) and $160,000 (for parents filing jointly). Those making slightly more may receive a smaller tax credit, but once income goes above $90,000 (for a single parent) and $180,000 (for parents filing jointly), your parents won't qualify for the credit at all. Anyone earning more than those amounts is not eligible for this tax credit.

By the way, if you are an emancipated student who files their own tax return, no one claims you as a dependent, and you're paying your way through college, you are likely eligible for these credits. You are also eligible for something called a Lifetime Learning Credit on your taxes.

As stated by the IRS: "For the tax year, you may be able to claim a lifetime learning credit of up to $2,000 for qualified education expenses paid for all eligible students. There is no limit on the number of years the lifetime learning credit can be claimed for each student."[2]

Once you start paying tuition to a college or university, you can expect to receive Tax Form 1098-T from your college. This shows the IRS exactly how much you spent paying for college, based on money you sent to your school. It also shows any scholarships or financial aid you received directly from your school. You'll need this tax form if you are going to file to receive the American Opportunity Tax Credit. Again, the expenses you did not pay directly to your school could be applicable for the American Opportunity Tax Credit as well. Make sure you keep receipts for all of those expenses.

If you're unsure how to handle college-related expenses or the tax forms you receive when doing your tax return, I strongly suggest you speak with a certified public accountant or an enrolled agent. These are both professionals you can hire to help with tax returns. If you've always done your taxes yourself, once you've got college expenses to consider, it might be time to bring an expert tax preparer onboard.

Coupons and shopping apps

An obvious way to save money at college is to use coupons. I'm not telling you something you don't already know. However, what you might not know is that there are plenty of coupon apps you can use on your smartphone. Some of our favorites are the kinds that give you cash back for scanning your store receipt, such as Ibotta and Receipt Hog.

That said, there are plenty of traditional paper coupons that can save you big time. For example, the drugstore nearest my youngest daughter's college campus is CVS. The CVS rewards program is called Extra Bucks, and my daughter has become an Extra Bucks queen. She tells me that, on average, she can save 50 percent on what she buys at CVS. My older daughter's nearest drugstore is Duane Reade, part of the Walgreens family. She collects points as part of the Balance Rewards program that the chain offers, and cashes them in to get a discount on her purchases as well.

Don't think coupons or cash back apps are worth it? According to Valassis, a company that provides coupon inserts in newspapers, Americans collectively save about $3 billion a year by using coupons. Valassis also says that the majority of Americans who use coupons save between $30 and $50 per week.[3]

Chapter 13

Freebies and Discounts
for College Students

In Chapter 12: Savings on College Supplies, I talked about ways you can save money on your everyday supplies. These were the kind of supplies you need for going to class and studying for those classes, in your dorm room, apartment, or at the library. Much of that chapter was devoted to savings on textbooks because, let's face it, if there's one thing that college students need, it's college textbooks.

In this chapter we are focusing on more of the fun stuff, that is, free things that students can enjoy just because they are college students. This could be free food, clothing, or entertainment that's available on or near college campuses. If freebies aren't forthcoming, there are always student discounts. You wouldn't believe how many places nationwide will lop off 10 percent or more of your bill just because you showed your student ID. Finally, I'll provide options for savings on health expenses when you're at school. Okay, so that health stuff may not be as "fun" as the free stuff, but it's worth mentioning nonetheless.

Discounts and freebies with your student ID

Remember in Chapter 12 how I talked about Amazon Prime Student being 50 percent less than a regular Prime account? That's because you're a student and have that .edu e-mail address to prove it. That .edu address is as good as any student ID you might show in a physical store.

Amazon is hardly the only website, store, restaurant, or business willing to knock a little off your tab just because you're a student. I've tracked down 18 categories and some specific business names within each that offer legit student discounts. Note: some stores even offer discounts to high school students. So if your high school issues a student ID, you can get started enjoying these discounts now.

It goes without saying, by the way, that you should do your own due diligence and double check that these offers still exist or that conditions haven't changed since this book was published. Hopefully, they won't have changed, but I would hate for you to be all excited about saving money and then end up disappointed when you get to the checkout counter. Finally, you may have read my article on this topic on Parade.com. The information in this chapter offers much more detail than that original story.

Clothing retailers

Lots of brick-and-mortar stores that attract college-aged shoppers will give students a discount. All you have to do is show your college ID. In my research, I found that most stores offer a 15 percent discount. Also, this discount is often limited to full-priced merchandise only. So if you were hoping to stack the discount with something on clearance, you're out of luck.

Some retailers that give students a discount include J.Crew, Banana Republic, and TopShop. Even some thrift stores give a student discount. The Goodwill stores near me have designated Saturday as student discount day. You should find out if the Goodwill stores near you have a similar discount day for students. This is good to know if you like to go thrift store shopping, because it allows you to save even more on their incredibly cheap prices.

Restaurants

Many eateries located near college campuses will offer some kind of discount for students. On a chain level, I know that Chipotle and Zaxby's offer special student discounts on a certain day of the week or month of the year. Because many chains are franchised—meaning individuals own one or more locations versus a national company owning every single location—these owners might choose to offer discounts that you might not find at another restaurant in the same chain. For example, I have heard of student discounts at Arby's, McDonald's, and Subway, but could not confirm it at the corporate level. So this is yet another reason to ask locally if that discount applies to a restaurant near your campus.

Travel companies

If you need to take a train home, to a job interview, or to visit a friend, you should know that Amtrak has a student advantage card that gets you 15 percent off fares. The catch is you have to book at least three days in advance and, I imagine, there is a limit to the number of fares eligible for this discount. Nonetheless, if you can plan ahead, you may just save 15 percent on your train ticket.

If you commute to school via train or bus, you could get a discount on your daily ticket. New Jersey Transit, for example, has a student pass that provides a 25 percent discount on a monthly ticket. The student pass web page lists more than 60 colleges in New York and New Jersey that, if you attend one of these schools, you're eligible to save on your monthly train, bus, or light rail ticket. Other commuter rail or bus lines may offer similar discounts near where you live or where you'll attend school. I recommend searching using the phrase "student pass" or "student discount" plus the name of the transportation company.

Speaking of buses, Greyhound offers student discounts as well—10 percent off tickets. However, you need have something called the Student Advantage Card, which I've explained in the following box. Megabus also offers student discounts. Finally, Bolt Bus, another cheap means of transportation that college students favor, doesn't have a student discount, per se. However, it does have a rewards program. After taking eight trips on the bus, you've earned a free one-way ticket. So that's something worth noting.

If you happen to be traveling in Europe or Canada while in college, don't forget your student ID there. Both Rail Europe, which owns Eurail, and VIA Rail Canada, have student discounts.

Student discount membership program

You may find that some of the discounts for students are linked to something called a Student Advantage Card. This is a card you buy for $20 each year, and then you're eligible for discounts on everything from travel (Greyhound bus tickets and Lyft ride-shares) to shopping (*www.Target.com* and *www.Footlocker.com*). According to the Student Advantage Card website, the company that runs the card has also negotiated discounts at local restaurants and stores on or near college campuses. Before you plunk down the $20, though, do some research around campus to see how many places actually take the card, and what kind of savings you might get. I want you to be sure that you can easily recoup the $20 investment.

Digital products and apps

You already know that Amazon Prime Student has become the go-to service for college students looking to save on textbooks, get two-day free shipping, and enjoy free streaming music and video. Another streaming service with a student discount is Spotify. For about $5 a month, which is half the regular Spotify Premium rate, you'll get ad-free music that you can download and listen to even when you're offline.

As far as apps go, there are plenty of free apps that you can download and use on your smartphone. But what about an app that earns you discounts on food, clothing, and more, just for being a responsible student? And when I say responsible, I mean putting your phone away while in class. Here is one such app.

My daughter told me about Pocket Points, which encourages students not to touch their phones in class. Basically, you download the app, activate it when you get to class, and as long as you don't touch your phone while the app is on, you'll be earning points—about one point per 20 minutes of inactivity. That might not sound like a lot, but in a typical week, my daughter earns about 30 points. At 35 points, she would be able to get a free cookie at Insomnia Cookies, a place college students love to go to in order to satisfy late-night munchies. Other restaurants that have partnered with Pocket Points include Jersey Mike's Subs and Smoothie King. Some retailers and restaurants let you cash in for a discount or freebie with as little as 10 points earned.

Discounted magazine and newspaper subscriptions

College students who want to stay up to date with traditional newspaper or magazine subscriptions can find free and heavily discounted offers on campus or online. Look for flyers in your student center. At the same time, you can also go online to sign up for reduced-price subscriptions. For example, through the WSJ Student program, students can get the *Wall Street Journal* for only $49 a year. That's more than 50 percent off. Also, if you do end up with that Amazon Prime Student account, you can use it to get discounts on subscriptions as well, including the *Washington Post*, which the head of Amazon.com, Jeff Bezos, happens to own.

Tech and software

If your parents are planning on buying you a new computer before you head off to college, make sure you tell them about Apple's education discount. You can save at least $300 on a new laptop. Apple lets students *accepted* to college use this discount, too, so maybe you want to ask for that new computer for graduation.

What if yours isn't a Mac family? Well, you can find education discounts on other devices as well. Best Buy has a student program that helps you save between $50 and $100 on new computers, including the Microsoft Surface. The Microsoft Store offers similar discounts on its own products.

You may also save money on a new computer by calling your college's bookstore and finding out what prices they offer. Also, something to keep in mind if you do get a new computer is that your college may be able to hook you up with a suite of Microsoft Office products for free. So find out about this first before buying the software on your own.

Speaking of software, there are also student discounts on Adobe products but, like with Microsoft Office, wait to buy anything. If you'll be pursuing a major with specific software requirements, those "fees" you pay to the college could cover the cost of the software you'll need.

Gym membership

There is a very good chance that when you get to college, you'll find that you can work out at your campus gym for free. Your campus gym may even offer specialty classes at rock-bottom prices. My own daughters have spent $40 a semester for unlimited spinning, kickboxing, and yoga classes at their respective on-campus gyms.

Even so, you may find that *your* college fitness center isn't all that you want it to be. Don't stress. You may find a nearby chain fitness center, yoga studio, or CrossFit facility you can use and which might also have a student discount program. You'll never know unless you ask.

Health, counseling, and dental services

Whether you opt out of your college's health insurance or not, all students can use campus health services. In addition, if you need counseling services, you're likely to be able to take care of your mental health for free or really cheap. Finally, if you're attending a university with a dental school attached to it, look into free or reduced-cost dental checkups in their clinic. When my husband was a graduate student at the University of Michigan, and we were living on his paltry grad student teaching salary, we visited the University of Michigan School of Dentistry student dental clinics for our oral care. Although our dental checkups were not free, the fee we paid was significantly less than what we would have paid at a private dentist.

Financial services

College may be the first time in your life that you need to open a checking account, especially if you're hoping to have a debit card to use to pay for everyday expenses. When you go to the bank to open that checking account, make sure you ask about a student checking account. These usually do not have any of the regular fees that banks charge, such as ATM surcharges or check charges. If you're lucky, you might even get a freebie for opening a student checking account. My own daughters received a $50 bonus each.

Another financial services benefit for students is rewards for good grades. For example, if you're using Discover for your student loans, be sure to submit your transcript at the end of the school year. Discover gives students with good grades free money. That is, if you maintain a 3.0 GPA, Discover will give you a rebate worth 1 percent of your student loan. This is a one-time bonus, but if you have multiple Discover Student Loans, you can file for a bonus for each loan.

Q&A

Q: My bank charges a fee when I use another bank's ATM. There aren't any locations near where I'm going to college. What should I do?

A: When you open a bank account, I always recommend asking about ATM fee reimbursement. This is important if you have your money in a locally based bank that may not have ATMs near your college. If you're charged $3 or more each time you take out cash, then that can really add up. But many smaller banks *will* reimburse these fees, sometimes only up to a certain amount each month. For banks that will not reimburse withdrawal fees, here's a trick for getting your money for free: use your debit card at a store that offers a cash-back option at the checkout counter when you make a purchase.

Hair services

Though neither Sephora nor Ulta offer student discounts, your local beauty salon might. In fact, the place where my daughters and I get our haircut offers a 10 percent discount for student customers. It's not something they advertise, but when the receptionist heard my girls talking about going back to campus, she offered it to us. Find out if your local salon has a similar student discount.

Museum admission

When you go to college in New York City like I did, the cultural opportunities are endless. One of the benefits of being a New York college student was free admission to many of the city's museums. It turns out that this student benefit isn't just limited to museums in the Big Apple.

Many museums give students free admission, with a student ID, on a certain day of the week. Some colleges even have their own museum program (a separate card) that gets you in for free at a whole host of museums in your city. Check with the student life, student affairs, or a similar office at your school about how you might be able to get into museums for free.

Movie tickets

Most of the major movie chains have some sort of student discount. Sometimes the discount is limited to a certain day of the week. Other times only certain movies have a student discount price associated with them. So you'll have to confirm if your local Regal, AMC, or Cinemark movie theater offers discounts. Definitely call first before making your plans or buying tickets on Fandango.

Theater tickets

If you're lucky enough to attend school in a place with a thriving theater community, you're likely to score tickets for free or really cheap. Probably the best place to get these discounted theater tickets is the student activities office on campus. If that's not an option, you can always check with individual theaters and shows to see if they have a student discount.

Another option if you're going to college in and around New York City is the Theatre Development Fund (TDF) at *www.tdf.org*. This nonprofit provides discounted theater tickets to students, educators, civil servants, and others. Membership costs just $30 a year. Membership gets you access to Broadway tickets for as little as $9. Even if you're not going to school near New York City, if you know you'll be visiting at some point in your school career, the $30 membership fee might be worth it.

Auto insurance

Many college students are still on mom and dad's auto insurance policy. I know my daughters are. If that describes you, let your parents know this: if you get good grades in school, they can get a discount on auto insurance. This is true with GEICO, Allstate, and State Farm. If you're covering your own auto insurance, these same companies may even offer discounted policies for students.

Sporting events

If you go to a school with good sporting teams, then I'm sure you'll be attending football, basketball, and other sporting events—possibly even for free. Even so, if your college is near a city with major league or national franchise teams, find out if you can get a student discount on tickets. Teams that currently offer such a discount include the Boston Red Sox and the Pittsburgh Pirates.

Moving services

Your parents will likely move you into and out of college. But if you're moving without mom and dad around, you can probably encourage your friends to help for free by paying them in pizza. Even so, if you need a legit mover or at least a legit moving truck, check out Budget and Penske truck rentals. Both offer college discounts as high as 20 percent off.

Printing and shipping services

When it comes time to look for internships or full-time jobs, you'll need to print up resumes and business cards.

www.Moo.com offers discounts throughout the year just for students. I've gotten business cards from Moo in the past. They're awesome. Plus, as a student, you can save as much as 30 percent on an order.

Ski sports

College students who go to school near the slopes are going to love this. Some local tourism groups have put together discounted ski packages or lift tickets for students. The College New England Pass, for example, is a season pass that costs $1,000 *less* than the most expensive season pass.

Another option is to check with individual ski resorts near your campus about discounts. There may be days of the week or times of the day when you can pay a reduced price to ski or snowboard.

Sign up for e-mail clubs

Do you want a surefire way to get restaurant freebies and discounts, regardless of your academic status? Sign up for a restaurant's e-mail club as well as any rewards program it might offer. Usually, when you sign up, you'll receive a coupon to save on a meal purchase or for a BOGO (buy one get one free) offer. Additionally, many e-mail clubs ask for your birthday. Don't forget to include it. Why? That's because around the time of your birthday, the restaurant will e-mail you with some kind of free offer. I know this firsthand. During my birthday month, I've received an e-mailed coupon from Panera Bread for a free cookie or free cup of coffee, and an e-mailed coupon from Jersey Mike's for a free fountain drink.

Save on student health insurance

Do you want to know how my daughters have saved $3,000 and $2,000 each year on college costs? They opted out of the required student health insurance plan at their respective colleges because they have insurance through their parents—us.

If you'll recall from Chapter 9, Ann Logue's family was able to save $2,600 because of their decision around son Drew's health insurance while in college. That is, Drew attends college in Canada, where universal health insurance is required. It costs them about $600 per year. At the same time, because he was covered by his Canadian health insurance, his parents were able to drop him from their paid health insurance plan, thus saving them $2,600 overall.

Why colleges require health insurance

Not every college and university requires students to have health insurance. At first it was just public university systems that enacted this health insurance requirement. Many private colleges joined in after the Affordable Care Act became law. As of this writing, the new administration is reconsidering the future of the ACA, so student health insurance requirements could be changing significantly in the near future. Even so, I imagine that private colleges such as the ones my daughters attend will not change their health insurance requirements going forward. So this money-saving tip will still apply.

Changes in Washington aside, at first glance you might think that requiring students to have health insurance is a money-making scheme. Colleges get to charge you an extra fee on top of tuition, room and board, and whatever other fees you may be paying to go to college there. Although there may be some truth to the attractiveness of profit to be made from making students buy the college insurance plan if they do not have health insurance otherwise, the bottom line may not actually be about the bottom line in an entirely sinister way.

Students with health insurance tend to take better care of themselves. Because they do not have to worry about the cost of seeing a doctor, they're more likely to actually go to the doctor or student health services when they are sick. Students who get the care they need are less likely to become so ill that they cannot finish their studies. In other words, the students stay healthy, make it to their classes, and can graduate on time. It looks really good for college rankings when students graduate on time.

Should you opt out of health insurance?

In my opinion, if you can have the option for health insurance while you're in college and you're not otherwise already insured, you should take it. But if your parents are already paying for health insurance and you're on their plan, there's no reason to pay for health insurance through your school.

Keep in mind that most colleges require you to renew your health insurance every academic year. Some make you renew every semester. That means that you will need to waive or opt out of health insurance before the beginning of the fall and spring semesters if you want to save money each year.

I'm thankful we have health insurance and can provide coverage for our daughters while they pursue their education. But I'm really thankful for the fact that, by opting out of college insurance, during four years of college, my daughters will have saved us, collectively, $20,000.

Notes

Introduction

1. "Are you in the American middle class? Find out with our income calculator," by Richard Fry and Rakesh Kochhar, May 11, 2016 Pew Research Center, http://pewresearch.org/fact-tank/2016/05/11/are-you-in-the-american-middle-class/.

Chapter 1

1. Georgetown University Public Policy Institute study, "Recovery: Job Growth and Education Requirements Through 2020" by Anthony Carnevale, Nicole Smith, and Jeff Strohl, Center on Education and the Workforce, McCourt School of Public Policy, Georgetown University, June 26, 2013, https://cew.georgetown.edu/cew-reports/recovery-job-growth-and-education-requirements-through-2020/.

2. "The Rising Cost of Not Going to College" by Pew Research Center, February 11, 2014, http://pewsocialtrends.org/2014/02/11/the-rising-cost-of-not-going-to-college/.

3. Employment Situation Summary Table A. Household data, seasonally adjusted, Bureau of Labor Statistics, https://bls.gov/news.release/empsit.a.htm. (Note: the number I cite in the text was current as of the writing of the book. It has since changed and will change every month as the data is updated monthly.)

4. "Alumnifire Launches Digital Networking Platform That Allows Alumni To Give Back To Their Network With Something More Than Money," press release, May 19, 2015, http://prweb.com/releases/2015/05/prweb12730149.htm.

5. "Checking in on Alumni Sentiments: Corporate Insight Survey Reveals Link Between Alumni Engagement and College Fundraising," press release from Corporate Insight, November 23,

2015, http://prnewswire.com/news-releases/
checking-in-on-alumni-sentiments-corporate-
insight-survey-reveals-link-between-alumni-
engagement-and-college-fundraising-300182861.
html.

Chapter 2

1. "Financial Aid FAQs from The College Board,"
   https://bigfuture.collegeboard.org/pay-for-college/
   financial-aid-101/financial-aid-faqs.

2. "Parents, You're Paying for College Wrong," by
   Catey Hill, Marketwatch, July 31, 2014, http://
   marketwatch.com/story/parents-youre-paying-for-
   college-wrong-2014-07-31.

3. Source: The Consumer Financial Protection
   Bureau is a government agency built to protect
   consumers, https://consumerfinance.gov/askcfpb/
   search/?selected_facets=category_exact:credit-
   reporting.

4. Florida Prepaid Tuition website, http://
   myfloridaprepaid.com/what-we-offer/.

Chapter 3

1. The 2014 Consumer Financial Literacy Survey.
   Prepared for: The National Foundation for
   Credit Counseling (NFCC). Prepared by:
   Harris Poll, https://nfcc.org/NewsRoom/
   FinancialLiteracy/files2013/NFCC_2014Fin
   ancialLiteracySurvey_datasheet_and_key_
   findings_031314%20FINAL.pdf.

2. "Drivers Can Save an Average of $859 a Year by Comparing Car Insurance Rates," by Jeffrey Chu, November 10, 2015, https://nerdwallet.com/blog/insurance/compare-car-insurance-save-859-a-year/.

3. https://consumer.ftc.gov/articles/0145-settling-credit-card-debt.

Chapter 4

1. https://apstudent.collegeboard.org/apcourse.

2. https://apstudent.collegeboard.org/takingtheexam/exam-fees.

3. Tuition costs of colleges and universities, National Center for Education Statistics, part of the U.S. Department of Education, https://nces.ed.gov/fastfacts/display.asp?id=76.

4. Student Score Distributions AP Exams—May 2016 from The College Board, https://research.collegeboard.org/programs/ap/data/participation/ap-2016.

5. https://enrollment.rochester.edu/ib/.

6. https://scad.edu/admission/admission-information/freshman/international-baccalaureate-credit.

7. https://ciachef.edu/transfer-credit-policies/.

Chapter 5

1. https://nces.ed.gov/datatools/.

2. Table 317.20. Degree-granting postsecondary institutions, by control and level of institution and state or jurisdiction: 2014–15 National Center for Education Statistics, https://nces. ed.gov/programs/digest/d15/tables/dt15_317.20. asp?current=yes.

3. https://aau.edu/sites/default/files/AAU%20Files/ Key%20Issues/Taxation%20%26%20Finance/ Section-117-d-Qualified-Tuition-Reduction-FINAL.pdf.

4. *College and University Professional Association for Human Resources* 2010 Comprehensive Survey of College and University Benefits Programs Survey Fact Sheet, https://cupahr.org/surveys/ files/Benefits10-Survey-Fact-Sheet.pdf.

Chapter 6

1. Chapter 1: College applications, State of College Admission report from the National Association for College Admission Counseling, https:// nacacnet.org/news--publications/publications/ state-of-college-admission/soca-chapter1/.

2. 2015 State of College Admission Report, page 15, National Association for College Admission Counseling. You can download the report from this page: https://nacacnet.org/news--publications/ publications/state-of-college-admission/ soca-download/.

Chapter 8

1. Corporation for National and Community Service, https://nationalservice. gov/programs/americorps/alumni/ segal-americorps-education-award.

Chapter 9

1. "Community College FAQs," Community College Research Center, Teachers College, Columbia University, http://ccrc.tc.columbia.edu/ Community-College-FAQs.html.

2. "Fast Facts from Our Fact Sheet," American Association of Community Colleges, http://aacc. nche.edu/AboutCC/Pages/fastfactsfactsheet.aspx.

3. "Americans are moving to Europe for free college degrees," by Katie Lobosco, February 23, 2016, http://money.cnn.com/2016/02/23/pf/ college/free-college-europe/.

4. https://studyinnorway.no/study-in-norway/ Tuition; http://english.hi.is/university/ applications; Foreign Students in Germany 2012, report downloaded from the Federal Ministry of Education and Research, Germany, https://bmbf. de/en/index.html.

Chapter 11

1. "How America Pays for College 2016, A snapshot of the national study," by Sallie Mae

and Ipsos, https://salliemae.com/research/
how-america-pays-for-college/.

Chapter 12

1. https://irs.gov/publications/p970/ch03.html.
2. https://irs.gov/individuals/aotc.
3. "Today's Coupon Users 2016," by Valassis, http://
   valassis.com/resources/infographics/item/160824/
   todays-coupon-users. Total coupon savings,
   Consumers Save $3.6 Billion by Redeeming
   Coupons in 2014 *Food and Non-Food Marketers
   Strategically use Media Mix to Manage Coupon
   Value Increases*, Livonia, Mich., Feb. 12, 2015,
   https://nchmarketing.com/NCH_Website/
   News_and_Events/Press_Releases/2015_
   Press_Releases/Consumers_Save_$3_6_
   Billion_By_Redeeming_Coupons_In_2014_
   (February_2015)/.

Resource Hacks

Throughout this book I've mentioned services, companies, and websites that can help you on your quest to save money while paying for college. In this Resource Hacks section, I've compiled most of the major recommendations from the book, along with a brief description, and where you can go online to get more information. I'm hoping this makes it easier for you to come back to this one place and get the details you need so you can check out something for yourself or visit a website to learn more. I've listed the resources below in alphabetical order.

Please keep in mind that URLs included below were accurate, working, and up to date when I was writing this book.

Advanced Placement (AP) Classes

The College Board, the same people who do the SATs, is responsible for AP classes and for administering the exams. Students can use AP classes to earn the equivalent of college credits while still in high school.

https://apstudent.collegeboard.org/

Alabama Prepaid Affordable College Tuition (PACT) Program

PACT is the state of Alabama's prepaid tuition program.

http://treasury.alabama.gov/pact/

Amazon Prime Student

Amazon Prime Student is a reduced-cost version of a Prime account that offers students two-day free shipping on purchases.

www.amazon.com

American Opportunity Tax Credit

The American Opportunity Tax Credit allows expenses paid for tuition, certain fees, and course materials for higher education to be claimed through the tax year 2017 (or the income tax return you would file in 2018).

You can use this tax credit for the first four years of a college education only.

https://www.irs.gov/individuals/aotc

Barnes & Noble Textbook Rentals

Barnes & Noble Textbook Rentals allow you to rent textbooks through your college bookstore or online.

http://www.barnesandnoble.com/h/textbooks/rental

Bonner Scholars

Bonner Scholars is a service-based program that provides financial aid at more than 60 colleges nationwide.

http://www.bonner.org/

California-Oregon Reciprocity

California and Oregon offer a tuition reciprocity program that focuses on tuition discounts at California community colleges and attendance at Southern Oregon University in Ashland, Oregon. There isn't a singular website with information about the agreement. However, the participating colleges have a page on their websites about it, such as this one for Southern Oregon University:

http://www2.sou.edu/admissions/afford/california/califoregon-reciprocity-agreements/

Catholic College Cooperative Tuition Exchange

More than 70 Catholic colleges participate in this tuition exchange.

http://cccte.org/

The Chronicle of Higher Education

This is a trade publication for people who work in higher education. It's a great resource for looking for jobs in higher education.

http://www.chronicle.com/

CIC Tuition Exchange Program

Through the Council of Independent Colleges, a group of smaller, often religious-affiliated schools, more than 430 colleges and universities participate in the CIC Tuition Exchange.

https://www.cic.edu/member-services/tuition-exchange-program

The New England Pass

This provides discounted lift tickets and ski packages to college students in New England.

http://www.newenglandpass.com/

Common Application

The Common Application, a.k.a. the Common App, is a website that nearly 700 colleges and universities in the United States and worldwide belong to, which allows students to go to one place online to apply to multiple colleges.

https://www.commonapp.org/

College Illinois 529 Prepaid Tuition Plan
College Illinois is the state's prepaid tuition plan.
http://www.collegeillinois.org/

Consumer Financial Protection Bureau (CFPB)
The CFPB is a government agency formed in 2008 after the financial crisis to help educate consumers on financial matters.
https://www.consumerfinance.gov/

CSS Profile
The CSS Profile is another college financial aid form. CSS stands for College Scholarship Service. It's most popular with private colleges.
https://student.collegeboard.org/css-financial-aid-profile

DC Tuition Assistance Grant (DCTAG)
Through the DC Tuition Assistance Grant (DCTAG), you can apply to receive a discounted tuition rate at state colleges and universities in any of the 50 states, plus Guam and Puerto Rico.
https://osse.dc.gov/dctag

Direct Loan Program
There are multiple kinds of loans in the Direct Loan Program, a federal loan program for parents and students to help them pay for a college education.
https://studentaid.ed.gov/sa/types/loans

Equifax

Equifax is a consumer credit reporting agency, and is one of the top three used in the United States. You are allowed to contact them once a year to get your free credit report.

https://equifax.com/personal/

Experian

Experian is a consumer credit reporting agency, and is one of the top three used in the United States. You are allowed to contact them once a year to get your free credit report.

http://www.experian.com/

FAFSA

FAFSA stands for the Free Application for Federal Student Aid. Every college student should complete the FAFSA every year, even if you believe your family makes too much money to qualify for financial aid. It's the only way you can get federal loans to pay for college.

https://fafsa.ed.gov/

Fastweb

Fastweb aggregates information, and delivers it to your inbox on a regular basis, based on the student profile you've created on the site.

https://www.fastweb.com/

Florida Bright Futures

Florida Bright Futures scholarship program provides a full ride to state institutions.

http://www.floridastudentfinancialaid.org/ssfad/bf/

Florida Prepaid

Florida Prepaid is the state's prepaid tuition program, which includes an option for prepaying room and board.

http://www.myfloridaprepaid.com/

Georgia Hope Programs

Georgia Hope Programs is actually a somewhat generic term to describe a number of scholarship programs available to Georgia high school students.

https://gsfc.georgia.gov/hope

Guaranteed Education Tuition (Washington State)

Guaranteed Education Tuition, or GET, is Washington State's 529 prepaid college tuition plan.

http://www.get.wa.gov/

Higher Ed Jobs

This is a higher-education job site that, along with faculty openings, lists non-academic jobs, such as those in food services, childcare services, and police and public safety.

https://www.higheredjobs.com/

Insider Higher Ed

This is a trade magazine for those who work at colleges and universities. It has a free-to-use job search tool.

https://www.insidehighered.com/

Internal Revenue Service (IRS)

There are many tax-related questions with regards to paying for college. A great resource is the IRS website.

https://www.irs.gov/

The International Baccalaureate (IB) Program

This is a curriculum offered by some high schools that allows high school students to earn college credit for their IB test scores.

http://ibo.org/

Jack Kent Cooke Foundation

This foundation provides scholarships for all college students, including undergraduates looking to transfer, either from community or another four-year college.

http://www.jkcf.org/

Maryland 529

Maryland 529 administers the Maryland prepaid tuition program.

https://maryland529.com/

Michigan Education Trust

Michigan Education Trust is Michigan's 529 prepaid tuition plan.

http://www.michigan.gov/setwithmet/

The Midwest Student Exchange Program (MSEP)

MSEP covers nine states in the Midwest that allows students to receive in-state tuition at a neighboring state's schools.

http://msep.mhec.org/

Minnesota-Wisconsin Tuition Reciprocity

Minnesota-Wisconsin Tuition Reciprocity covers reciprocal tuition agreements at state colleges and universities in both Wisconsin and Minnesota.

http://www.heab.state.wi.us/reciprocity/

The Mississippi Prepaid Affordable College Tuition Plan (MPACT)

MPACT is Mississippi's prepaid tuition plan that prepays the cost of college tuition and mandatory fees.

http://www.treasurerlynnfitch.ms.gov/collegesavingsmississippi/Pages/MPACT.aspx

Moo.com

This is a high-quality business card printing company with a student discount.

https://www.moo.com/us/

Nevada Prepaid Tuition Program

This is Nevada's prepaid tuition plan.

http://www.nevadatreasurer.gov/Prepaid_Tuition/Prepaid_Home/

New England Regional Student Program (RSP)

The RSP "Tuition Break" allows residents in the six New England states to receive in-state tuition, under certain circumstances, in other New England states.

http://www.nebhe.org/programs-overview/rsp-tuition-break/overview/

New Jersey (NJ) Transit Student Pass

The NJ Transit Student Pass web page lists more than 60 colleges and universities in the New York and New Jersey area. If you're a student at one of these schools and commute to class, you can save 25 percent on a monthly ticket for the train, bus, or light rail systems that NJ Transit runs.

http://njtransit.com/ti/ti_servlet.srv?hdnPageAction=StudentPassTo

New Mexico-Colorado Tuition Reciprocity

Colorado college students who want to attend school in New Mexico—and conversely, New Mexico students wanting to attend school in Colorado—will be granted in-state tuition at participating public colleges.

https://www.unm.edu/~unmreg/reciprocal.htm

Ohio Tuition Reciprocity

The Ohio Tuition Reciprocity program includes a specific list of schools in four neighboring states where Ohio residents can enjoy in-state tuition.

https://www.ohiohighered.org/tuition-reciprocity

Perkins Loans

Perkins Loans are a federal loan program for students who have financial need. Many middle-class students can end up qualifying for Perkins Loans.

https://studentaid.ed.gov/sa/types/loans/perkins

Phi Theta Kappa

This is the community college honor society. If you earn Phi Theta Kappa membership while in community college, you can apply for and possibly receive up to $30,000 in scholarships.

http://www.ptk.org/

Pocket Points

Pocket Points is an app you can download to your smartphone. It encourages students not to touch their phones in class. You activate the app when you get to class, and as long as you don't touch your phone while the app is on, you earn one point for every 20 minutes or so of inactivity. At 10 points earned, you can start getting discounts and freebies at restaurants and retailers.

https://pocketpoints.com/

Robertson Scholars Leadership Program

The Robertson Scholars Leadership Program exists at two North Carolina colleges—Duke University and the University of North Carolina-Chapel Hill—and offers full-ride scholarships.

https://robertsonscholars.org/

Southern Regional Education Board (SREB) Academic Common Market

The SREB Academic Common Market is a consortium of more than 100 colleges and universities in 15 states that offer in-state tuition to out-of-state students looking to get a degree not offered in their home state.

https://www.sreb.org/academic-common-market

The Stamps Family Charitable Foundation

Stamps Scholars receive full-tuition scholarships and is available at more than 40 colleges and universities nationwide.

http://www.stampsfoundation.org/

Student Advantage Card

You spend $20 each year for the Student Advantage Card, and then you're eligible for discounts on everything from travel (Greyhound bus tickets and Lyft rideshares) to shopping (Target.com and Footlocker.com).

https://studentadvantage.com/discountcard/

Texas Tuition Promise Fund

Texas Tuition Promise Fund is Texas' prepaid tuition plan.

http://texastomorrowfunds.org/

Theatre Development Fund (TDF)

This nonprofit provides discounted theater tickets to students. A $30 per year membership fee provides access to Broadway tickets for as little as $9.

https://www.tdf.org/

TransUnion

TransUnion is a consumer credit reporting agency, and is one of the top three used in the United States. You are allowed to contact them once a year to get your free credit report.

https://www.transunion.com/

The Tuition Exchange

This is a program that more than 660 major college and universities use for reciprocal tuition exchanges.

http://www.tuitionexchange.org/

U.Plan Prepaid Tuition Program (Massachusetts)

U.Plan is the Commonwealth of Massachusetts' prepaid tuition program, which is good at both public and private colleges and universities in Massachusetts.

https://www.mefa.org/products/u-plan/

U.S. Department of Education's Financial Aid Website

This is a site where you can get more information about all the different loans available to students and parents to help pay for your education.

http://studentaid.ed.gov

U.S. Department of Education Office of Postsecondary Education

Search the U.S. Department of Education's Office of Postsecondary Education's database to find out if a college or university is accredited or not.

https://ope.ed.gov/accreditation/

University of Maine Flagship Match Program

The University of Maine Flagship Match Program guarantees that students from certain states who meet a certain academic criteria will pay the same in-state tuition as the flagship state university in their home state.

https://go.umaine.edu/apply/scholarships/flagship-match/

<u>University of Minnesota Reciprocity Program</u>

Through the University of Minnesota Reciprocity Program, residents of three states and one Canadian province can apply to pay in-state tuition at one of the University of Minnesota's five campuses.

https://onestop.umn.edu/finances/reciprocity-programs

<u>Vanderbilt Ingram Scholars</u>

More than 40 students each year receive full rides as Vanderbilt Ingram Scholars at Vanderbilt University.

http://vanderbilt.edu/ingram/

<u>Virginia 529 Prepaid</u>

Virginia 529 Prepaid is the Commonwealth of Virginia's prepaid tuition program.

https://www.virginia529.com/

<u>The Western Undergraduate Exchange (WUE)</u>

WUE is a regional program offering tuition reciprocity for students in more than a dozen Western states to receive in-state tuition in other Western states.

http://wiche.edu/wue

Index

About the Author

Leah Ingram, aka The Confident Spender, has been showing people how to be smart with their money for more than a decade, helping thousands of people, regardless of their age or income, feel good about their finances.

A regular contributor to Parade.com, her work has also appeared in *AARP*, *Good Housekeeping*, and many other publications. Ingram is the author of 15 books and holds a degree in journalism from New York University.

For more information, visit *www.LeahIngram.com*.